The Order for the Celebration of
Holy Communion
also called
The Eucharist
and
The Lord's Supper

CHURCH HOUSE
PUBLISHING

Church House Publishing
Church House
Great Smith Street
London SW1P 3NZ

ISBN   0-7151-3835 9

Published 2000 for the Archbishops' Council
by Church House Publishing

Telephone   020 7898 1557
Fax   020 7898 1449
Email   copyright@c-of-e.org.uk

Printed by   University Printing House, Cambridge

Designed by   Derek Birdsall RDI

Typeset by   John Morgan & Shirley Birdsall / Omnific

Publisher's note   The layout and design of this booklet give an indication
of the intended appearance of *Common Worship*, but are not
necessarily identical in every respect with the final published
version at the end of 2000 (for example, the pagination will
be different). Some texts referred to in the rubrics (for example,
the Apostles' Creed) are not in this booklet; they will appear
elsewhere in the main volume of *Common Worship*.

Contents

sample

Introduction to this sample edition

These services of Holy Communion are being issued now so
that people may have the chance to study them and reflect in each
worshipping community on how to prepare for their introduction
at the end of the year.

There are two Orders of Holy Communion, each in both
contemporary and traditional language. Order One has the shape
and structure of the revised rites that led to Rite A in the ASB,
which is now common to the rites of all the major churches in
the western tradition. Order Two has the shape and structure of
the rite in *The Book of Common Prayer*.

In Order One, the rite is presented first in contemporary and then
in traditional language. The structure is the same and is outlined
on page 17. The order of service on pages 19 to 35 (pages 59 to 79
in traditional language) contains all the texts regularly spoken by
the whole assembly and all the rubrics needed to follow the service.
Exactly the same is true for Order Two, with the structure outlined
on page 81, and the order in traditional language on pages 83 to 98
(pages 103 to 120 in contemporary language).

The pattern for Order One has four main sections:

¶ *The Gathering*, during which the assembly is constituted by singing or
saying together the opening prayers, is recalled in penitence to its
baptismal status, and is prepared to receive the Word of God.
This section is summed up in the presidential Collect.

¶ *The Liturgy of the Word*, during which the assembly engages with the
Word, as the story of what God has done in Christ is set
alongside the community's experience, and in the Sermon the
implications are teased out for prayer and action.

¶ *The Liturgy of the Sacrament*, during which the assembly is offered the
possibility of transformation as it is incorporated into the one,
perfect self-offering of Christ to the Father and receives the body
and blood of Christ in faith with thanksgiving.

¶ *The Dismissal*, when the assembly is reminded to put into practice
the new life it has received, and is sent out into the community
to do so.

In Order Two these elements are equally clear, though presented
differently.

As each worshipping community takes this opportunity to think afresh about the nature of the Eucharist and its place within the life of the parish and the Church's mission, you may wish to consider how to present your worship, reflecting on

¶ the history and worshipping tradition of the church
¶ the availability of different musical resources
¶ the way in which the ordering of the church building has developed
¶ the relationship of the church to the community it serves.

As you review the particular opportunities of the local community and its history, it is important to set that in the wider context of the theology and development of our worship, and in particular

¶ the theology of the Eucharist in the Church
¶ the history and development of the celebration of the Eucharist
¶ what it is that this community wishes to emphasize as it celebrates the Eucharist.

As you decide which version to use, these questions may help you reflect:

¶ how much variety is desirable and sustainable in each worshipping community?
¶ how will you present the celebration so that the deep structure of the rite is clear?
¶ how will you try to secure a different feel for the Eucharist at different seasons or on different days – on a weekday in Lent, Easter Day, All Saints' Day or a Sunday in Advent, for example?
¶ which of the variable prayers – especially the eucharistic prayers – and which of the optional alternatives in the supplementary texts will you use, and on which occasions?
¶ how are you going to interpret what the Notes say about the appropriate roles for ministers in relation to the assembly?
¶ how are you going to encourage the use of the Form of Preparation in helping worshippers prepare for the service?

However you tackle these important issues, our hope in publishing this sample edition is that you will be encouraged to begin to pray these services as you study them, so that when they become authorized for use, the Church's eucharistic worship may move seamlessly into *Common Worship* from Advent 2000.

✠ David Sarum
Chairman of the Liturgical Commission

sample

¶ General Notes

¶ Preparation

Careful devotional preparation before the service is recommended for every communicant. A Form of Preparation for public or private use is provided (page 11).

¶ Ministries

Holy Communion is celebrated by the whole people of God gathered for worship. The ministry of the members of the congregation is expressed through their active participation together in the words and actions of the service, but also by some of them reading the Scripture passages, leading the prayers of intercession, and, if authorized, assisting with the distribution of Communion.

In some traditions the ministry of the deacon at Holy Communion has included some of the following elements: the bringing in of the Book of the Gospels, the invitation to confession, the reading of the Gospel, the preaching of the sermon when licensed to do so, a part in the prayers of intercession, the preparation of the table and the gifts, a part in the distribution, the ablutions and the dismissal.

The deacon's liturgical ministry provides an appropriate model for the ministry of an assisting priest, a Reader, or another episcopally authorized minister in a leadership ministry that complements that of the president.

The unity of the liturgy is served by the ministry of the president, who in presiding over the whole service holds word and sacrament together and draws the congregation into a worshipping community.

The president at Holy Communion (who, in accordance with the provisions of Canon B 12 'Of the Ministry of the Holy Communion', must have been episcopally ordained priest), expresses this ministry by saying the opening Greeting, the Absolution, the Collect, the Peace and the Blessing. The president must say the Eucharistic Prayer, break the consecrated bread and receive the sacrament on every occasion. When appropriate, the president may, after greeting the people, delegate the leadership of all or parts of the Gathering and the Liturgy of the Word to a deacon, Reader or other authorized lay person.

In the absence of a priest for the first part of the service, a deacon, Reader or other authorized lay person may lead the entire Gathering and Liturgy of the Word.

When the bishop is present, he normally presides over the whole service.

As provided in Canon B 18 the sermon shall be preached by a duly authorized minister, deaconess, Reader or lay worker or, at the invitation of the minister having the cure of souls and with the permission of the bishop, another person.

¶ **Communicant members of other Churches**

Baptized persons who are communicant members of other Churches which subscribe to the doctrine of the Holy Trinity and are in good standing in their own Church shall be admitted to Communion in accordance with Canon B 15A.

For further notes, see pages 184–9.

A Form of Preparation

This form may be used in any of three ways.

It may be used by individuals as part of their preparation for Holy Communion.

It may be used corporately on suitable occasions within Holy Communion where it replaces the sections entitled 'Prayer of Preparation' and 'Prayers of Penitence'.

It may be used as a separate service of preparation. When used in this way, there should be added at the beginning a greeting and at the end the Peace and the Lord's Prayer. Hymns, psalms and other suitable liturgical material may also be included.

Come, Holy Ghost *(Veni Creator Spiritus)*

All   **Come, Holy Ghost, our souls inspire,**
And lighten with celestial fire;
Thou the anointing Spirit art,
Who dost thy sevenfold gifts impart.

Thy blessed unction from above
Is comfort, life and fire of love;
Enable with perpetual light
The dullness of our blinded sight.

Anoint and cheer our soiled face
With the abundance of thy grace;
Keep far our foes, give peace at home;
Where thou art guide no ill can come.

Teach us to know the Father, Son,
And thee, of Both, to be but One;
That through the ages all along
This may be our endless song:

Praise to thy eternal merit,
Father, Son and Holy Spirit.
Amen.

sample

Exhortation

As we gather at the Lord's table we must recall the promises and
warnings given to us in the Scriptures and so examine ourselves and
repent of our sins. We should give thanks to God for his redemption
of the world through his Son Jesus Christ and, as we remember
Christ's death for us and receive the pledge of his love, resolve
to serve him in holiness and righteousness all the days of our life.

The Commandments

Hear the commandments which God has given to his people,
and examine your hearts.

I am the Lord your God: you shall have no other gods but me.

All **Amen. Lord, have mercy.**

You shall not make for yourself any idol.

All **Amen. Lord, have mercy.**

You shall not dishonour the name of the Lord your God.

All **Amen. Lord, have mercy.**

Remember the Sabbath and keep it holy.

All **Amen. Lord, have mercy.**

Honour your father and your mother.

All **Amen. Lord, have mercy.**

You shall not commit murder.

All **Amen. Lord, have mercy.**

You shall not commit adultery.

All **Amen. Lord, have mercy.**

You shall not steal.

All **Amen. Lord, have mercy.**

You shall not bear false witness against your neighbour.

All **Amen. Lord, have mercy.**

You shall not covet anything which belongs to your neighbour.

All **Amen. Lord, have mercy upon us
and write all these your laws in our hearts.**

Or one of the forms of the Commandments in the Supplementary Texts (pages 123–5) may be used.

Or, in place of the Commandments, one of these texts may be used.

Summary of the Law

Our Lord Jesus Christ said:
The first commandment is this:
'Hear, O Israel, the Lord our God is the only Lord.
You shall love the Lord your God with all your heart,
with all your soul, with all your mind,
and with all your strength.'

The second is this: 'Love your neighbour as yourself.'
There is no other commandment greater than these.
On these two commandments hang all the law and the prophets.

All **Amen. Lord, have mercy.**

(or)

The Comfortable Words

Hear the words of comfort our Saviour Christ says
to all who truly turn to him:

Come to me, all who labour and are heavy laden,
and I will give you rest.   *Matthew 11.28*

God so loved the world that he gave his only-begotten Son,
that whoever believes in him should not perish
but have eternal life.   *John 3.16*

Hear what Saint Paul says:
This saying is true, and worthy of full acceptance,
that Christ Jesus came into the world to save sinners. *1 Timothy 1.15*

Hear what Saint John says:
If anyone sins, we have an advocate with the Father,
Jesus Christ the righteous;
and he is the propitiation for our sins.   *1 John 2.1-2*

(or)

The Beatitudes

Let us hear our Lord's blessing on those who follow him.

Blessed are the poor in spirit,
for theirs is the kingdom of heaven.

Blessed are those who mourn,
for they shall be comforted.

Blessed are the meek,
for they shall inherit the earth.

Blessed are those who hunger and thirst after righteousness,
for they shall be satisfied.

Blessed are the merciful,
for they shall obtain mercy.

Blessed are the pure in heart,
for they shall see God.

Blessed are the peacemakers,
for they shall be called children of God.

Blessed are those who suffer persecution for righteousness' sake,
for theirs is the kingdom of heaven.

Silence for Reflection

Confession

All **Father eternal, giver of light and grace,**
we have sinned against you and against our neighbour,
in what we have thought,
in what we have said and done,
through ignorance, through weakness,
through our own deliberate fault.
We have wounded your love,
and marred your image in us.
We are sorry and ashamed,
and repent of all our sins.
For the sake of your Son Jesus Christ,
who died for us,
forgive us all that is past,
and lead us out from darkness
to walk as children of light.
Amen.

or another authorized confession may be used.

Absolution

Almighty God, our heavenly Father,
who in his great mercy
has promised forgiveness of sins
to all those who with heartfelt repentance and true faith
turn to him:
have mercy on *you*;
pardon and deliver *you* from all *your* sins;
confirm and strengthen *you* in all goodness;
and bring *you* to everlasting life;
through Jesus Christ our Lord.

All **Amen.**

Order One   *Structure*

The people and the priest

gathering {
¶ greet each other in the Lord's name

¶ confess their sins and are assured of God's forgiveness

¶ keep silence and pray a collect
}

liturgy of the word {
¶ proclaim and respond to the word of God

¶ pray for the Church and the world
}

liturgy of the sacrament {
¶ exchange the Peace

¶ prepare the table

¶ pray the Eucharistic Prayer

¶ break the bread

¶ receive communion
}

Dismissal ¶ depart with God's blessing

For Notes, see page 184.

sample

Order One

¶ *The Gathering*

At the entry of the ministers a hymn may be sung.

The president may say

In the name of the Father,
and of the Son,
and of the Holy Spirit.

All **Amen.**

The Greeting

The president greets the people

The Lord be with you

All **and also with you.**

(or)

Grace, mercy and peace
from God our Father
and the Lord Jesus Christ
be with you

All **and also with you.**

From Easter Day to Pentecost this acclamation follows

Alleluia. Christ is risen.

All **He is risen indeed. Alleluia.**

Words of welcome or introduction may be said.

sample

Prayer of Preparation

This prayer may be said

All **Almighty God,**
to whom all hearts are open,
all desires known,
and from whom no secrets are hidden:
cleanse the thoughts of our hearts
by the inspiration of your Holy Spirit,
that we may perfectly love you,
and worthily magnify your holy name;
through Christ our Lord.
Amen.

Prayers of Penitence

The Commandments, the Beatitudes, the Comfortable Words or the following Summary of the Law may be used

Our Lord Jesus Christ said:
The first commandment is this:
'Hear, O Israel, the Lord our God is the only Lord.
You shall love the Lord your God with all your heart,
with all your soul, with all your mind,
and with all your strength.'

The second is this: 'Love your neighbour as yourself.'
There is no other commandment greater than these.
On these two commandments hang all the law and the prophets.

All **Amen. Lord, have mercy.**

A minister uses a seasonal invitation to confession or these or other suitable words

God so loved the world
that he gave his only Son Jesus Christ
to save us from our sins,
to be our advocate in heaven,
and to bring us to eternal life.

Let us confess our sins in penitence and faith,
firmly resolved to keep God's commandments
and to live in love and peace with all.

All **Almighty God, our heavenly Father,**
we have sinned against you
and against our neighbour
in thought and word and deed,
through negligence, through weakness,
through our own deliberate fault.
We are truly sorry
and repent of all our sins.
For the sake of your Son Jesus Christ,
who died for us,
forgive us all that is past,
and grant that we may serve you in newness of life
to the glory of your name.
Amen.

(or)

All **Most merciful God,**
Father of our Lord Jesus Christ,
we confess that we have sinned
in thought, word and deed.
We have not loved you with our whole heart.
We have not loved our neighbours as ourselves.
In your mercy
forgive what we have been,
help us to amend what we are,
and direct what we shall be;
that we may do justly,
love mercy,
and walk humbly with you, our God.
Amen.

sample

Or, with suitable penitential sentences, the Kyrie Eleison may be used

Lord, have mercy.

All **Lord, have mercy.**

Christ, have mercy.

All **Christ, have mercy.**

Lord, have mercy.

All **Lord, have mercy.**

If another confession has already been used, the Kyrie Eleison may be used without interpolation here or after the absolution.

The president says

Almighty God,
who forgives all who truly repent,
have mercy upon *you*,
pardon and deliver *you* from all *your* sins,
confirm and strengthen *you* in all goodness,
and keep *you* in life eternal;
through Jesus Christ our Lord.

All **Amen.**

Gloria in Excelsis

Gloria in Excelsis may be used

All **Glory to God in the highest,**
and peace to his people on earth.

Lord God, heavenly King,
almighty God and Father,
we worship you, we give you thanks,
we praise you for your glory.

Lord Jesus Christ, only Son of the Father,
Lord God, Lamb of God,
you take away the sin of the world:
have mercy on us;
you are seated at the right hand of the Father:
receive our prayer.

For you alone are the Holy One,
you alone are the Lord,
you alone are the Most High, Jesus Christ,
with the Holy Spirit,
in the glory of God the Father.
Amen.

The Collect

The president introduces a period of silent prayer with the words
'Let us pray' or a more specific bidding.

The Collect is said, and all respond

All **Amen.**

sample

¶ *The Liturgy of the Word*

Readings

Either one or two readings from Scripture precede the Gospel reading.

At the end of each the reader may say

This is the word of the Lord.

All **Thanks be to God.**

The psalm or canticle follows the first reading; other hymns and songs may be used between the readings.

Gospel Reading

An acclamation may herald the Gospel reading.

When the Gospel is announced the reader says

Hear the Gospel of our Lord Jesus Christ according to N.

All **Glory to you, O Lord.**

At the end

This is the Gospel of the Lord.

All **Praise to you, O Christ.**

Sermon

The Creed

*On Sundays and principal holy days an authorized translation of
the Nicene Creed is used, or on occasion the Apostles' Creed or
an authorized affirmation of faith may be used (see pages 00–00).*

All **We believe in one God,
the Father, the almighty,
maker of heaven and earth,
of all that is,
seen and unseen.**

**We believe in one Lord, Jesus Christ,
the only Son of God,
eternally begotten of the Father,
God from God, Light from Light,
true God from true God,
begotten, not made,
of one Being with the Father;
through him all things were made.
For us and for our salvation he came down from heaven,**
was **he became incarnate from the Holy Spirit and the Virgin Mary
and was made man.
For our sake he was crucified under Pontius Pilate;
he suffered death and was buried.
On the third day he rose again
in accordance with the Scriptures;
he ascended into heaven
and is seated at the right hand of the Father.
He will come again in glory to judge the living and the dead,
and his kingdom will have no end.**

**We believe in the Holy Spirit,
the Lord, the giver of life,
who proceeds from the Father and the Son,
who with the Father and the Son is worshipped and glorified,
who has spoken through the prophets.
We believe in one holy catholic and apostolic Church.
We acknowledge one baptism for the forgiveness of sins.
We look for the resurrection of the dead,
and the life of the world to come.
Amen.**

sample

Prayers of Intercession

One of the forms on pages 135–41 or other suitable words may be used.

The prayers usually include these concerns and may follow this sequence:

¶ *The Church of Christ*

¶ *Creation, human society, the Sovereign and those in authority*

¶ *The local community*

¶ *Those who suffer*

¶ *The communion of saints*

These responses may be used

Lord, in your mercy
All **hear our prayer.**

(or)

Lord, hear us.
All **Lord, graciously hear us.**

And at the end

Merciful Father,
All **accept these prayers
for the sake of your Son,
our Saviour Jesus Christ.
Amen.**

¶ The Liturgy of the Sacrament

The Peace

The president may introduce the Peace with a suitable sentence, and then says

The peace of the Lord be always with you

All **and also with you.**

These words may be added
Let us offer one another a sign of peace.

All may exchange a sign of peace.

Preparation of the Table
Taking of the Bread and Wine

A hymn may be sung.

The gifts of the people may be gathered and presented.

The table is prepared and bread and wine are placed upon it.

One or more of the prayers at the preparation of the table may be said.

The president takes the bread and wine.

sample

The Eucharistic Prayer

An authorized Eucharistic Prayer is used.

The president says

The Lord be with you   *(or)*   The Lord is here.

All   **and also with you.**   **His Spirit is with us.**

Lift up your hearts.

All   **We lift them to the Lord.**

Let us give thanks to the Lord our God.

All   **It is right to give thanks and praise.**

The president praises God for his mighty acts and all respond

All   **Holy, holy, holy Lord,**
God of power and might,
heaven and earth are full of your glory.
Hosanna in the highest.
[Blessed is he who comes in the name of the Lord.
Hosanna in the highest.]

The president recalls the Last Supper,
and one of these four acclamations may be used

[Great is the mystery of faith:]   [Praise to you, Lord Jesus:]

All   **Christ has died:**   **Dying you destroyed**
Christ is risen: **our death,**
Christ will come again.   **rising you restored our life:**
                                     Lord Jesus, come in glory.

[Christ is the bread of life:]   [Jesus Christ is Lord:]

All   **When we eat this bread**   **Lord, by your cross and**
      and drink this cup,   **resurrection**
we proclaim your death,   **you have set us free.**
      Lord Jesus,   **You are the Saviour of the**
until you come in glory.   **world.**

The Prayer continues and leads into the doxology,
to which all respond boldly

All   **Amen.**

Prayer A

This response may be used

All **To you be glory and praise for ever.**

and the Prayer ends

All **Blessing and honour and glory and power
be yours for ever and ever.
Amen.**

Prayer D

These words are used

This is his/our story.

All **This is our song:
Hosanna in the highest.**

and the Prayer ends

All **Blessing and honour and glory and power
be yours for ever and ever.
Amen.**

Prayer F

These responses may be used

All **Amen. Lord, we believe.**

All **Amen. Come, Lord Jesus.**

All **Amen. Come, Holy Spirit.**

Prayer G

Prayer G ends

All **Blessing and honour and glory and power
be yours for ever and ever.
Amen.**

Prayer H

For Prayer H, see page 56.

sample

The Lord's Prayer

As our Saviour taught us, so we pray

All   **Our Father in heaven,**
hallowed be your name,
your kingdom come,
your will be done,
on earth as in heaven.
Give us today our daily bread.
Forgive us our sins
as we forgive those who sin against us.
Lead us not into temptation
but deliver us from evil.
For the kingdom, the power,
and the glory are yours
now and for ever.
Amen.

(or)

Let us pray with confidence as our Saviour has taught us

All   **Our Father, who art in heaven,**
hallowed be thy name;
thy kingdom come;
thy will be done;
on earth as it is in heaven.
Give us this day our daily bread.
And forgive us our trespasses,
as we forgive those who trespass against us.
And lead us not into temptation;
but deliver us from evil.
For thine is the kingdom,
the power and the glory,
for ever and ever.
Amen.

Breaking of the Bread

The president breaks the consecrated bread.

We break this bread
to share in the body of Christ.

All **Though we are many, we are one body,
because we all share in one bread.**

(or)

Every time we eat this bread
and drink this cup,

All **we proclaim the Lord's death
until he comes.**

Agnus Dei may be used as the bread is broken.

All **Lamb of God,
you take away the sin of the world,
have mercy on us.**

**Lamb of God,
you take away the sin of the world,
have mercy on us.**

**Lamb of God,
you take away the sin of the world,
grant us peace.**

(or)

All **Jesus, Lamb of God,
have mercy on us.**

**Jesus, bearer of our sins,
have mercy on us.**

**Jesus, redeemer of the world,
grant us peace.**

Giving of Communion

The president says one of these invitations to communion

Draw near with faith.
Receive the body of our Lord Jesus Christ
which he gave for you,
and his blood which he shed for you.
Eat and drink
in remembrance that he died for you,
and feed on him in your hearts
by faith with thanksgiving.

(or)

Jesus is the Lamb of God
who takes away the sin of the world.
Blessed are those who are called to his supper.

All **Lord, I am not worthy to receive you,
but only say the word, and I shall be healed.**

(or)

God's holy gifts
for God's holy people.

All **Jesus Christ is holy,
Jesus Christ is Lord,
to the glory of God the Father.**

or, from Easter Day to Pentecost

Alleluia. Christ our passover is sacrificed for us.

All **Therefore let us keep the feast. Alleluia.**

One of these prayers may be said before the distribution

All **We do not presume**
to come to this your table, merciful Lord,
trusting in our own righteousness,
but in your manifold and great mercies.
We are not worthy
so much as to gather up the crumbs under your table.
But you are the same Lord
whose nature is always to have mercy.
Grant us, therefore, gracious Lord,
so to eat the flesh of your dear Son Jesus Christ
and to drink his blood,
that our sinful bodies may be made clean by his body
and our souls washed through his most precious blood,
and that we may evermore dwell in him, and he in us.
Amen.

(or)

All **Most merciful Lord,**
your love compels us to come in.
Our hands were unclean,
our hearts were unprepared;
we were not fit
even to eat the crumbs from under your table.
But you, Lord, are the God of our salvation,
and share your bread with sinners.
So cleanse and feed us
with the precious body and blood of your Son,
that he may live in us and we in him;
and that we, with the whole company of Christ,
may sit and eat in your kingdom.
Amen.

The president and people receive communion.

Authorized words of distribution are used and the communicant replies

Amen.

During the distribution hymns and anthems may be sung.

sample

If either or both of the consecrated elements are likely to prove insufficient, the president returns to the holy table and adds more, saying the words on page 150.

Any consecrated bread and wine which is not required for purposes of communion is consumed at the end of the distribution or after the service.

Prayer after Communion

Silence is kept.

The post communion or another suitable prayer is said.

All may say one of these prayers

All   **Almighty God,**
we thank you for feeding us
with the body and blood of your Son Jesus Christ.
Through him we offer you our souls and bodies
to be a living sacrifice.
Send us out
in the power of your Spirit
to live and work
to your praise and glory.
Amen.

(or)

All   **Father of all,**
we give you thanks and praise,
that when we were still far off
you met us in your Son and brought us home.
Dying and living, he declared your love,
gave us grace, and opened the gate of glory.
May we who share Christ's body live his risen life;
we who drink his cup bring life to others;
we whom the Spirit lights give light to the world.
Keep us firm in the hope you have set before us,
so we and all your children shall be free,
and the whole earth live to praise your name;
through Christ our Lord.
Amen.

¶ The Dismissal

A hymn may be sung.

The president may use the seasonal blessing, or another suitable blessing

(or)

The peace of God,
which passes all understanding,
keep your hearts and minds
in the knowledge and love of God,
and of his Son Jesus Christ our Lord;
and the blessing of God almighty,
the Father, the Son, and the Holy Spirit,
be among you and remain with you always.

All **Amen.**

A minister says

Go in peace to love and serve the Lord.
All **In the name of Christ. Amen.**

(or)

Go in the peace of Christ.
All **Thanks be to God.**

or, from Easter Day to Pentecost

Go in the peace of Christ. Alleluia, Alleluia.
All **Thanks be to God. Alleluia, Alleluia.**

The ministers and people depart.

sample

¶ *Eucharistic Prayers for use in Order One*

Proper prefaces are to be found on pages 148 and 154–83.

Prayer A

Euchanistic Prayers 4 2 blended - 8 grially - reflect Sch. 2

If an extended preface (pages 148 and 154–83) is used, it replaces all words between the opening dialogue and the Sanctus.

The Lord be with you   *(or)*   The Lord is here.

All   **and also with you.**   **His Spirit is with us.**

Lift up your hearts.

All   **We lift them to the Lord.**

Let us give thanks to the Lord our God.

All   **It is right to give thanks and praise.**

It is indeed right,
it is our duty and our joy,
at all times and in all places
to give you thanks and praise,
holy Father, heavenly King,
almighty and eternal God,
through Jesus Christ your Son our Lord.

The following may be omitted if a short proper preface is used

For he is your living Word;
through him you have created all things from the beginning,
and formed us in your own image.

[*All*   **To you be glory and praise for ever.**]

Through him you have freed us from the slavery of sin,
giving him to be born of a woman and to die upon the cross;
you raised him from the dead
and exalted him to your right hand on high.

[*All*   **To you be glory and praise for ever.**]

Through him you have sent upon us
your holy and life-giving Spirit,
and made us a people for your own possession.

[*All*   **To you be glory and praise for ever.**]

Short proper preface, when appropriate

Therefore with angels and archangels,
and with all the company of heaven,
we proclaim your great and glorious name,
for ever praising you and *saying:*

All **Holy, holy, holy Lord,**
God of power and might,
heaven and earth are full of your glory.
Hosanna in the highest.
[Blessed is he who comes in the name of the Lord.
Hosanna in the highest.]

Accept our praises, heavenly Father,
through your Son our Saviour Jesus Christ,
and as we follow his example and obey his command,
grant that by the power of your Holy Spirit
these gifts of bread and wine
may be to us his body and his blood;

who, in the same night that he was betrayed,
took bread and gave you thanks;
he broke it and gave it to his disciples, saying:
Take, eat; this is my body which is given for you;
do this in remembrance of me.

[All **To you be glory and praise for ever.]**

In the same way, after supper
he took the cup and gave you thanks;
he gave it to them, saying:
Drink this, all of you;
this is my blood of the new covenant,
which is shed for you and for many for the forgiveness of sins.
Do this, as often as you drink it,
in remembrance of me.

[All **To you be glory and praise for ever.]**

Therefore, heavenly Father,
we remember his offering of himself
made once for all upon the cross;
we proclaim his mighty resurrection and glorious ascension;
we look for the coming of your kingdom,
and with this bread and this cup
we make the memorial of Christ your Son our Lord.

One of the following is used.

[Great is the mystery of faith:]

All **Christ has died:**
Christ is risen:
Christ will come again.

(or)

[Praise to you, Lord Jesus:]

All **Dying you destroyed our death,**
rising you restored our life:
Lord Jesus, come in glory.

(or)

[Christ is the bread of life:]

All **When we eat this bread and drink this cup,**
we proclaim your death, Lord Jesus,
until you come in glory.

(or)

[Jesus Christ is Lord:]

All **Lord, by your cross and resurrection**
you have set us free.
You are the Saviour of the world.

Accept through him, our great high priest,
this our sacrifice of thanks and praise,
and as we eat and drink these holy gifts
in the presence of your divine majesty,
renew us by your Spirit,
inspire us with your love
and unite us in the body of your Son,
Jesus Christ our Lord.

[*All*   **To you be glory and praise for ever.**]

Through him, and with him, and in him,
in the unity of the Holy Spirit,
with all who stand before you in earth and heaven,
we worship you, Father almighty,
in songs of everlasting praise:

All   **Blessing and honour and glory and power
be yours for ever and ever.
Amen.**

The service continues with the Lord's Prayer on page 30.

Prayer B

Euch. Prayer 3 (handwritten)

If an extended preface (pages 148 and 154–83) is used, it replaces all words between the opening dialogue and the Sanctus. *Hippolytus* (handwritten)

The Lord be with you	*(or)* The Lord is here.
All **and also with you.**	**His Spirit is with us.**

Lift up your hearts.
All **We lift them to the Lord.**

Let us give thanks to the Lord our God.
All **It is right to give thanks and praise.**

Father, we give you thanks and praise
through your beloved Son Jesus Christ, your living Word,
through whom you have created all things;
who was sent by you in your great goodness to be our Saviour.

By the power of the Holy Spirit he took flesh;
as your Son, born of the blessed Virgin,
he lived on earth and went about among us;
he opened wide his arms for us on the cross;
he put an end to death by dying for us;
and revealed the resurrection by rising to new life;
so he fulfilled your will and won for you a holy people.

Short proper preface, when appropriate

Therefore with angels and archangels,
and with all the company of heaven,
we proclaim your great and glorious name,
for ever praising you and *saying*:

All **Holy, holy, holy Lord,**
God of power and might,
heaven and earth are full of your glory.
Hosanna in the highest.
[Blessed is he who comes in the name of the Lord.
Hosanna in the highest.]

Lord, you are holy indeed, the source of all holiness;
grant that by the power of your Holy Spirit,
and according to your holy will,
these gifts of bread and wine
may be to us the body and blood of our Lord Jesus Christ;

who, in the same night that he was betrayed,
took bread and gave you thanks;
he broke it and gave it to his disciples, saying:
Take, eat; this is my body which is given for you;
do this in remembrance of me.

In the same way, after supper
he took the cup and gave you thanks;
he gave it to them, saying:
Drink this, all of you;
this is my blood of the new covenant,
which is shed for you and for many for the forgiveness of sins.
Do this, as often as you drink it,
in remembrance of me.

One of the following is used

[Great is the mystery of faith:]
All **Christ has died:**
Christ is risen:
Christ will come again.

(or)

[Praise to you, Lord Jesus:]
All **Dying you destroyed our death,**
rising you restored our life:
Lord Jesus, come in glory.

(or)

[Christ is the bread of life:]
All **When we eat this bread and drink this cup,**
we proclaim your death, Lord Jesus,
until you come in glory.

(or)

[Jesus Christ is Lord:]
All **Lord, by your cross and resurrection**
you have set us free.
You are the Saviour of the world.

sample

And so, Father, calling to mind his death on the cross,
his perfect sacrifice made once for the sins of the whole world;
rejoicing in his mighty resurrection and glorious ascension,
and looking for his coming in glory,
we celebrate this memorial of our redemption.
As we offer you this our sacrifice of praise and thanksgiving,
we bring before you this bread and this cup
and we thank you for counting us worthy
to stand in your presence and serve you.

Send the Holy Spirit on your people
and gather into one in your kingdom
all who share this one bread and one cup,
so that we, in the company of (*N and*) all the saints,
may praise and glorify you for ever,
through Jesus Christ our Lord;

by whom, and with whom, and in whom,
in the unity of the Holy Spirit,
all honour and glory be yours, almighty Father,
for ever and ever.

All **Amen.**

The service continues with the Lord's Prayer on page 30.

Prayer C

(handwritten: BCP resonances – old series 1 – Cranmer)

The Lord be with you   *(or)*   The Lord is here.

All **and also with you.**   **His Spirit is with us.**

Lift up your hearts.

All **We lift them to the Lord.**

Let us give thanks to the Lord our God.

All **It is right to give thanks and praise.**

It is indeed right,
it is our duty and our joy,
at all times and in all places
to give you thanks and praise,
holy Father, heavenly King,
almighty and eternal God,
through Jesus Christ our Lord:

Short proper preface, when appropriate

[or, when there is no proper preface

For he is our great high priest,
who has loosed us from our sins
and has made us to be a royal priesthood to you,
our God and Father.]

Therefore with angels and archangels,
and with all the company of heaven,
we proclaim your great and glorious name,
for ever praising you and *saying*:

All **Holy, holy, holy Lord,**
God of power and might,
heaven and earth are full of your glory.
Hosanna in the highest.
[Blessed is he who comes in the name of the Lord.
Hosanna in the highest.]

sample

All glory be to you, our heavenly Father,
who, in your tender mercy,
gave your only Son our Saviour Jesus Christ
to suffer death upon the cross for our redemption;
who made there by his one oblation of himself once offered
a full, perfect and sufficient sacrifice, oblation and satisfaction
    for the sins of the whole world;
he instituted, and in his holy gospel commanded us to continue,
a perpetual memory of his precious death until he comes again.

Hear us, merciful Father, we humbly pray,
and grant that, by the power of your Holy Spirit,
we receiving these gifts of your creation, this bread and this wine,
according to your Son our Saviour Jesus Christ's holy institution,
in remembrance of his death and passion,
may be partakers of his most blessed body and blood;

who, in the same night that he was betrayed,
took bread and gave you thanks;
he broke it and gave it to his disciples, saying:
Take, eat; this is my body which is given for you;
do this in remembrance of me.

In the same way, after supper
he took the cup and gave you thanks;
he gave it to them, saying:
Drink this, all of you;
this is my blood of the new covenant,
which is shed for you and for many for the forgiveness of sins.
Do this, as often as you drink it,
in remembrance of me.

One of these four acclamations is used

[Great is the mystery of faith:]

All **Christ has died:**
Christ is risen:
Christ will come again.

[Praise to you, Lord Jesus:]

Dying you destroyed
    our death,
rising you restored our life:
Lord Jesus, come in glory.

[Christ is the bread of life:]

All **When we eat this bread**
    and drink this cup,
we proclaim your death,
    Lord Jesus,
until you come in glory.

[Jesus Christ is Lord:]

Lord, by your cross and
    resurrection
you have set us free.
You are the Saviour of the
    world.

Therefore, Lord and heavenly Father,
in remembrance of the precious death and passion,
the mighty resurrection and glorious ascension
of your dear Son Jesus Christ,
we offer you through him this our sacrifice
    of praise and thanksgiving.

Grant that by his merits and death,
and through faith in his blood,
we and all your Church may receive forgiveness of our sins
and all other benefits of his passion.
Although we are unworthy, through our manifold sins,
to offer you any sacrifice,
yet we pray that you will accept this
the duty and service that we owe.
Do not weigh our merits, but pardon our offences,
and fill us all who share in this holy communion
with your grace and heavenly blessing;

through Jesus Christ our Lord,
by whom, and with whom, and in whom,
in the unity of the Holy Spirit,
all honour and glory be yours, almighty Father,
for ever and ever.

All   **Amen.**

The service continues with the Lord's Prayer on page 30.

sample

By James Jones - designed for use when chdn + young people present,
- what do we do w. our hands? See peach handout

Prayer D

The Lord be with you   *(or)*   The Lord is here.

All   **and also with you.**   **His Spirit is with us.**

Lift up your hearts.

All   **We lift them to the Lord.**

Let us give thanks to the Lord our God.

All   **It is right to give thanks and praise.**

Almighty God, good Father to us all,
your face is turned towards your world.
In love you gave us Jesus your Son
to rescue us from sin and death.
Your Word goes out to call us home
     to the city where angels sing your praise.
We join with them in heaven's song:

All   **Holy, holy, holy Lord,**
God of power and might,
heaven and earth are full of your glory.
Hosanna in the highest.
[Blessed is he who comes in the name of the Lord.
Hosanna in the highest.]

Father of all, we give you thanks
     for every gift that comes from heaven.

To the darkness Jesus came as your light.
With signs of faith and words of hope
he touched untouchables with love and washed the guilty clean.

This is his story.

All   **This is our song:**
Hosanna in the highest.

The crowds came out to see your Son,
     yet at the end they turned on him.
On the night he was betrayed
he came to table with his friends
     to celebrate the freedom of your people.

This is his story.

All   **This is our song:**
Hosanna in the highest.

Jesus blessed you, Father, for the food;
he took bread, gave thanks, broke it and said:
This is my body, given for you all.
Jesus then gave thanks for the wine;
he took the cup, gave it and said:
This is my blood, shed for you all
for the forgiveness of sins.
Do this in remembrance of me.

This is our story.

All **This is our song:**
Hosanna in the highest.

Therefore, Father, with this bread and this cup
we celebrate the cross
on which he died to set us free.
Defying death he rose again
and is alive with you to plead for us and all the world.

This is our story.

All **This is our song:**
Hosanna in the highest.

Send your Spirit on us now
that by these gifts we may feed on Christ
with opened eyes and hearts on fire.

May we and all who share this food
offer ourselves to live for you
and be welcomed at your feast in heaven
where all creation worships you,
Father, Son and Holy Spirit:

All **Blessing and honour and glory and power**
be yours for ever and ever.
Amen.

The service continues with the Lord's Prayer on page 30.

Prayer E

| | The Lord be with you | *(or)* | The Lord is here. |
| All | **and also with you.** | | **His Spirit is with us.** |

Lift up your hearts.

All   **We lift them to the Lord.**

Let us give thanks to the Lord our God.

All   **It is right to give thanks and praise.**

Here follows an extended preface (pages 148 and 154–83)
or the following

Father, you made the world and love your creation.
You gave your Son Jesus Christ to be our Saviour.
His dying and rising have set us free from sin and death.
And so we gladly thank you,
with saints and angels praising you, and *saying*:

All   **Holy, holy, holy Lord,**
God of power and might,
heaven and earth are full of your glory.
Hosanna in the highest.
[Blessed is he who comes in the name of the Lord.
Hosanna in the highest.]

We praise and bless you, loving Father,
through Jesus Christ, our Lord;
and as we obey his command,
send your Holy Spirit,
that broken bread and wine outpoured
may be for us the body and blood of your dear Son.

On the night before he died he had supper with his friends
and, taking bread, he praised you.
He broke the bread, gave it to them and said:
Take, eat; this is my body which is given for you;
do this in remembrance of me.

When supper was ended he took the cup of wine.
Again he praised you, gave it to them and said:
Drink this, all of you;
this is my blood of the new covenant,
which is shed for you and for many for the forgiveness of sins.
Do this, as often as you drink it, in remembrance of me.

So, Father, we remember all that Jesus did,
in him we plead with confidence his sacrifice
made once for all upon the cross.

Bringing before you the bread of life and cup of salvation,
we proclaim his death and resurrection
until he comes in glory.

One of these four acclamations is used

[Great is the mystery of faith:]

All **Christ has died:**
Christ is risen:
Christ will come again.

[Praise to you, Lord Jesus:]

Dying you destroyed
our death,
rising you restored our life:
Lord Jesus, come in glory.

[Christ is the bread of life:]

All **When we eat this bread**
and drink this cup,
we proclaim your death,
Lord Jesus,
until you come in glory.

[Jesus Christ is Lord:]

Lord, by your cross and
resurrection
you have set us free.
You are the Saviour of the
world.

Lord of all life,
help us to work together for that day
when your kingdom comes
and justice and mercy will be seen in all the earth.

Look with favour on your people,
gather us in your loving arms
and bring us with (*N and*) all the saints
to feast at your table in heaven.

Through Christ, and with Christ, and in Christ,
in the unity of the Holy Spirit,
all honour and glory are yours, O loving Father,
for ever and ever.

All **Amen.**

The service continues with the Lord's Prayer on page 30.

sample

Prayer F

	The Lord be with you	(or)	The Lord is here.
All	**and also with you.**		**His Spirit is with us.**

Lift up your hearts.

All **We lift them to the Lord.**

Let us give thanks to the Lord our God.

All **It is right to give thanks and praise.**

You are worthy of our thanks and praise
Lord God of truth,
for by the breath of your mouth
you have spoken your word,
and all things have come into being.

You fashioned us in your image
and placed us in the garden of your delight.
Though we chose the path of rebellion
you would not abandon your own.

Again and again you drew us into your covenant of grace.
You gave your people the law and taught us by your prophets
to look for your reign of justice, mercy and peace.

As we watch for the signs of your kingdom on earth,
we echo the song of the angels in heaven,
evermore praising you and *saying*:

All **Holy, holy, holy Lord,**
God of power and might,
heaven and earth are full of your glory.
Hosanna in the highest.
[Blessed is he who comes in the name of the Lord.
Hosanna in the highest.]

Lord God, you are the most holy one,
enthroned in splendour and light,
yet in the coming of your Son Jesus Christ
you reveal the power of your love
made perfect in our human weakness.

[All **Amen. Lord, we believe.]**

Embracing our humanity,
Jesus showed us the way of salvation;
loving us to the end,
he gave himself to death for us;
dying for his own,
he set us free from the bonds of sin,
that we might rise and reign with him in glory.

[*All*   **Amen. Lord, we believe.**]

On the night he gave up himself for us all
he took bread and gave you thanks;
he broke it and gave it to his disciples, saying:
Take, eat; this is my body which is given for you;
do this in remembrance of me.

[*All*   **Amen. Lord, we believe.**]

In the same way, after supper
he took the cup and gave you thanks;
he gave it to them, saying:
Drink this, all of you; this is my blood of the new covenant
which is shed for you and for many for the forgiveness of sins.
Do this, as often as you drink it, in remembrance of me.

[*All*   **Amen. Lord, we believe.**]

Therefore we proclaim the death that he suffered on the cross,
we celebrate his resurrection, his bursting from the tomb,
we rejoice that he reigns at your right hand on high
and we long for his coming in glory.

[*All*   **Amen. Come, Lord Jesus.**]

As we recall the one, perfect sacrifice of our redemption,
Father, by your Holy Spirit let these gifts of your creation
be to us the body and blood of our Lord Jesus Christ;
form us into the likeness of Christ
and make us a perfect offering in your sight.

[*All*   **Amen. Come, Holy Spirit.**]

sample

Look with favour on your people
and in your mercy hear the cry of our hearts.
Bless the earth,
heal the sick,
let the oppressed go free
and fill your Church with power from on high.

[*All*   **Amen. Come, Holy Spirit.**]

Gather your people from the ends of the earth
to feast with (*N and*) all your saints
at the table in your kingdom,
where the new creation is brought to perfection
in Jesus Christ our Lord;

by whom, and with whom, and in whom,
in the unity of the Holy Spirit,
all honour and glory be yours, almighty Father,
for ever and ever.

All   **Amen.**

The service continues with the Lord's Prayer on page 30.

-based on an RC eucharistic prayer.

Prayer G

The Lord be with you   *(or)*   The Lord is here.
All   **and also with you.**   **His Spirit is with us.**

Lift up your hearts.
All   **We lift them to the Lord.**

Let us give thanks to the Lord our God.
All   **It is right to give thanks and praise.**

Blessed are you, Lord God,
our light and our salvation;
to you be glory and praise for ever.

From the beginning you have created all things
and all your works echo the silent music of your praise.
In the fullness of time you made us in your image,
the crown of all creation.

You give us breath and speech, that with angels and archangels
and all the powers of heaven
we may find a voice to sing your praise:

All   **Holy, holy, holy Lord,**
God of power and might,
heaven and earth are full of your glory.
Hosanna in the highest.
[Blessed is he who comes in the name of the Lord.
Hosanna in the highest.]

How wonderful the work of your hands, O Lord.
As a mother tenderly gathers her children,
you embraced a people as your own.
When they turned away and rebelled
your love remained steadfast.

From them you raised up Jesus our Saviour, born of Mary,
to be the living bread,
in whom all our hungers are satisfied.

He offered his life for sinners,
and with a love stronger than death
he opened wide his arms on the cross.

sample

On the night before he died,
he came to supper with his friends
and, taking bread, he gave you thanks.
He broke it and gave it to them, saying:
Take, eat; this is my body which is given for you;
do this in remembrance of me.

At the end of supper, taking the cup of wine,
he gave you thanks, and said:
Drink this, all of you; this is my blood of the new covenant,
which is shed for you and for many for the forgiveness of sins.
Do this, as often as you drink it, in remembrance of me.

One of the following is used

[Great is the mystery of faith:]
All **Christ has died:**
Christ is risen:
Christ will come again.

(or)

[Praise to you, Lord Jesus:]
All **Dying you destroyed our death,**
rising you restored our life:
Lord Jesus, come in glory.

(or)

[Christ is the bread of life:]
All **When we eat this bread and drink this cup**
we proclaim your death, Lord Jesus,
until you come in glory.

(or)

[Jesus Christ is Lord:]
All **Lord, by your cross and resurrection**
you have set us free.
You are the Saviour of the world.

Father, we plead with confidence
his sacrifice made once for all upon the cross;
we remember his dying and rising in glory,
and we rejoice that he intercedes for us at your right hand.

Pour out your Holy Spirit as we bring before you
these gifts of your creation;
may they be for us the body and blood of your dear Son.

As we eat and drink these holy things in your presence,
form us in the likeness of Christ,
and build us into a living temple to your glory.

[Remember, Lord, your Church in every land.
Reveal her unity, guard her faith,
and preserve her in peace …]

*pray for Bishop. for sick, at
requiem - departed or bereaved, or
time of crisis.*

Bring us at the last with (*N and*) all the saints
to the vision of that eternal splendour
for which you have created us;
through Jesus Christ, our Lord,
by whom, with whom, and in whom,
with all who stand before you in earth and heaven,
we worship you, Father almighty, in songs of everlasting praise:

All **Blessing and honour and glory and power
be yours for ever and ever.
Amen.**

The service continues with the Lord's Prayer on page 30.

sample

- dependent on input of congregation to drive it along.
- language is simple & compressed
- not seasonal.
- don't restrict eucharistic diet to just this **Prayer H**

The Lord be with you *(or)* The Lord is here.

All **and also with you.** **His Spirit is with us.**

Lift up your hearts.

All **We lift them to the Lord.**

Let us give thanks to the Lord our God.

All **It is right to give thanks and praise.**

It is right to praise you, Father, Lord of all creation;
in your love you made us for yourself.

When we turned away
you did not reject us,
but came to meet us in your Son.

All **You embraced us as your children**
and welcomed us to sit and eat with you.

In Christ you shared our life
that we might live in him and he in us.

All **He opened his arms of love upon the cross**
and made for all the perfect sacrifice for sin.

On the night he was betrayed,
at supper with his friends
he took bread, and gave you thanks;
he broke it and gave it to them, saying:
Take, eat; this is my body which is given for you;
do this in remembrance of me.

All **Father, we do this in remembrance of him:**
his body is the bread of life.

At the end of supper, taking the cup of wine,
he gave you thanks, and said:
Drink this, all of you; this is my blood of the new covenant,
which is shed for you for the forgiveness of sins;
do this in remembrance of me.

All **Father, we do this in remembrance of him:**
his blood is shed for all.

As we proclaim his death and celebrate his rising in glory,
send your Holy Spirit that this bread and this wine
may be to us the body and blood of your dear Son.

All **As we eat and drink these holy gifts
make us one in Christ, our risen Lord.**

With your whole Church throughout the world
we offer you this sacrifice of praise
and lift our voice to join the eternal song of heaven:

All **Holy, holy, holy Lord,
God of power and might,
Heaven and earth are full of your glory.
Hosanna in the highest.**

The service continues with the Lord's Prayer on page 30.

sample

Order One *in Traditional Language*

¶ *The Gathering*

At the entry of the ministers a hymn may be sung.

The president may say

In the name of the Father,
and of the Son,
and of the Holy Spirit.

All **Amen.**

The Greeting

The president greets the people

The Lord be with you

All **and with thy spirit.**

(or)

Grace, mercy and peace
from God our Father
and the Lord Jesus Christ
be with you

All **and with thy spirit.**

From Easter Day to Pentecost this acclamation follows

Alleluia. Christ is risen.

All **He is risen indeed. Alleluia.**

Words of welcome or introduction may be said.

sample

Prayer of Preparation

This prayer may be said

All **Almighty God,**
unto whom all hearts be open,
all desires known,
and from whom no secrets are hid:
cleanse the thoughts of our hearts
by the inspiration of thy Holy Spirit,
that we may perfectly love thee,
and worthily magnify thy holy name;
through Christ our Lord.
Amen.

Prayers of Penitence

The Commandments, the Beatitudes, the Comfortable Words
or the following Summary of the Law may be used

Our Lord Jesus Christ said:
Hear, O Israel, the Lord our God is one Lord;
and thou shalt love the Lord thy God with all thy heart,
and with all thy soul, and with all thy mind,
and with all thy strength.
This is the first commandment.

And the second is like, namely this:
Thou shalt love thy neighbour as thyself.
There is none other commandment greater than these.
On these two commandments hang all the law and the prophets.

All **Lord, have mercy upon us, and write all these thy laws**
in our hearts, we beseech thee.

A minister uses a seasonal invitation to confession or these or other suitable words

God so loved the world
that he gave his only Son Jesus Christ
to save us from our sins,
to be our advocate in heaven,
and to bring us to eternal life.

Let us confess our sins in penitence and faith,
firmly resolved to keep God's commandments
and to live in love and peace with all.

All **Almighty God, our heavenly Father,**
we have sinned against thee
and against our neighbour,
in thought and word and deed,
through negligence, through weakness,
through our own deliberate fault.
We are heartily sorry
and repent of all our sins.
For the sake of thy Son Jesus Christ,
who died for us,
forgive us all that is past,
and grant that we may serve thee in newness of life
to the glory of thy name.
Amen.

(or)

All **Most merciful God,**
Father of our Lord Jesus Christ,
we confess that we have sinned
in thought, word and deed.
We have not loved thee with our whole heart.
We have not loved our neighbours as ourselves.
In thy mercy
forgive what we have been,
help us to amend what we are,
and direct what we shall be;
that we may do justly,
love mercy,
and walk humbly with thee, our God.
Amen.

sample

Or, with suitable penitential sentences, the Kyrie Eleison may be used

Lord, have mercy.

All   **Lord, have mercy.**

Christ, have mercy.

All   **Christ, have mercy.**

Lord, have mercy.

All   **Lord, have mercy.**

If another confession has already been used, the Kyrie Eleison may be used without interpolation here or after the absolution.

The president says

Almighty God,
who forgives all who truly repent,
have mercy upon *you*,
pardon and deliver *you* from all *your* sins,
confirm and strengthen *you* in all goodness,
and keep *you* in life eternal;
through Jesus Christ our Lord.

All   **Amen.**

Gloria in Excelsis

Gloria in Excelsis may be used

All **Glory be to God on high,**
and in earth peace, goodwill towards men.

We praise thee, we bless thee,
we worship thee, we glorify thee,
we give thanks to thee for thy great glory,
O Lord God, heavenly King,
God the Father almighty.

O Lord, the only-begotten Son, Jesus Christ:
O Lord God, Lamb of God, Son of the Father,
that takest away the sins of the world,
have mercy upon us.
Thou that takest away the sins of the world,
receive our prayer.
Thou that sittest at the right hand of God the Father,
have mercy upon us.

For thou only art holy;
thou only art the Lord;
thou only, O Christ,
with the Holy Ghost,
art the Most High,
in the glory of God the Father.
Amen.

The Collect

The president introduces a period of silent prayer with the words
'Let us pray' or a more specific bidding.

The Collect is said, and all respond

All **Amen.**

sample

¶ The Liturgy of the Word

Readings

*Either one or two readings from Scripture precede the
Gospel reading.*

At the end of each the reader may say

This is the word of the Lord.

All **Thanks be to God.**

*The psalm or canticle follows the first reading; other hymns and songs
may be used between the readings.*

Gospel Reading

An acclamation may herald the Gospel reading.

When the Gospel is announced, the reader says

Hear the Gospel of our Lord Jesus Christ according to *N.*

All **Glory be to thee, O Lord.**

At the end

This is the Gospel of the Lord.

All **Praise be to thee, O Christ.**

Sermon

The Creed

*On Sundays and principal holy days an authorized translation
of the Nicene Creed is used, or on occasion the Apostles' Creed
or an authorized affirmation of faith may be used (see pages 00–00).*

All **I believe in one God the Father almighty,
maker of heaven and earth,
and of all things
visible and invisible:**

**And in one Lord Jesus Christ,
the only-begotten Son of God,
begotten of his Father before all worlds,
God of God, Light of Light,
very God of very God,
begotten, not made,
being of one substance with the Father,
by whom all things were made;
who for us men and for our salvation
came down from heaven,
and was incarnate by the Holy Ghost of the Virgin Mary,
and was made man,
and was crucified also for us under Pontius Pilate.
He suffered and was buried,
and the third day he rose again
according to the Scriptures,
and ascended into heaven,
and sitteth on the right hand of the Father.
And he shall come again with glory
to judge both the quick and the dead:
whose kingdom shall have no end.**

**And I believe in the Holy Ghost,
the Lord, the giver of life,
who proceedeth from the Father and the Son,
who with the Father and the Son together
is worshipped and glorified,
who spake by the prophets.
And I believe one holy catholic and apostolic Church.
I acknowledge one baptism for the remission of sins.
And I look for the resurrection of the dead,
and the life of the world to come.
Amen.**

sample

Prayers of Intercession

One of the forms on pages 135–41 or other suitable words may be used.

The prayers usually include these concerns and may follow this sequence:

¶   *The Church of Christ*

¶   *Creation, human society, the Sovereign and those in authority*

¶   *The local community*

¶   *Those who suffer*

¶   *The communion of saints*

These responses may be used

Lord, in thy mercy
All   hear our prayer.

(or)

Lord, hear us.
All   Lord, graciously hear us.

And at the end

Merciful Father,
**All   accept these prayers
for the sake of thy Son,
our Saviour Jesus Christ.
Amen.**

¶ The Liturgy of the Sacrament

The Peace

The president may introduce the Peace with a suitable sentence, and then says

The peace of the Lord be always with you

All **and with thy spirit.**

These words may be added
Let us offer one another a sign of peace.

All may exchange a sign of peace.

Preparation of the Table
Taking of the Bread and Wine

A hymn may be sung.

The gifts of the people may be gathered and presented.

The table is prepared and bread and wine are placed upon it.

One or more of the prayers at the preparation of the table may be said.

The president takes the bread and wine.

The Eucharistic Prayer

One of the following Eucharistic Prayers is used:
Prayer A on page 68, Prayer C on page 71.

Prayer A

The Lord be with you   *(or)*   The Lord is here.
All **and with thy spirit.**   **His Spirit is with us.**

Lift up your hearts.
All **We lift them up unto the Lord.**

Let us give thanks to the Lord our God.
All **It is meet and right so to do.**

It is very meet, right and our bounden duty,
that we should at all times and in all places give thanks unto thee,
O Lord, holy Father,
almighty, everlasting God,
through Jesus Christ thine only Son our Lord.

The following may be omitted if a short proper preface is used

For he is thy living Word;
through him thou hast created all things from the beginning,
and fashioned us in thine own image.

Through him thou didst redeem us from the slavery of sin,
giving him to be born of a woman,
to die upon the cross,
and to rise again for us.

Through him thou hast made us a people for thine own possession,
exalting him to thy right hand on high,
and sending forth through him thy holy and life-giving Spirit.

Short proper preface, when appropriate

Therefore with angels and archangels,
and with all the company of heaven,
we laud and magnify thy glorious name,
evermore praising thee and *saying*:

All **Holy, holy, holy, Lord God of hosts,**
heaven and earth are full of thy glory.
Glory be to thee, O Lord most high.
[Blessed is he that cometh in the name of the Lord.
Hosanna in the highest.]

Accept our praises, heavenly Father,
through thy Son our Saviour Jesus Christ,
and as we follow his example and obey his command,
grant that by the power of thy Holy Spirit
these gifts of bread and wine
may be unto us his body and his blood;

who, in the same night that he was betrayed, took bread;
and when he had given thanks to thee,
he broke it and gave it to his disciples, saying:
Take, eat; this is my body which is given for you;
do this in remembrance of me.

Likewise after supper he took the cup;
and when he had given thanks to thee, he gave it to them, saying:
Drink ye all of this;
for this is my blood of the new covenant,
which is shed for you and for many for the forgiveness of sins.
Do this, as oft as ye shall drink it,
in remembrance of me.

Wherefore, O Lord and heavenly Father,
we remember his offering of himself
made once for all upon the cross;
we proclaim his mighty resurrection and glorious ascension;
we look for the coming of his kingdom
and with this bread and this cup
we make the memorial of Christ thy Son our Lord.

sample

One of the following may be used

[Great is the mystery of faith:]

All **Christ has died:**
Christ is risen:
Christ will come again.

(or)

[Jesus Christ is Lord:]

All **O Saviour of the world,**
who by thy cross and precious blood hast redeemed us,
save us, and help us, we humbly beseech thee, O Lord.

Accept through him, our great high priest,
this our sacrifice of thanks and praise,
and as we eat and drink these holy gifts
in the presence of thy divine majesty,
renew us by thy Holy Spirit,
inspire us with thy love,
and unite us in the body of thy Son,
Jesus Christ our Lord,

by whom, and with whom, and in whom,
in the unity of the Holy Spirit,
all honour and glory be unto thee,
O Father almighty,
world without end.

All **Amen.**

The service continues with the Lord's Prayer on page 74.

Prayer C

The Lord be with you   *(or)*   The Lord is here.
All   **and with thy spirit.**   **His Spirit is with us.**

Lift up your hearts.
All   **We lift them up unto the Lord.**

Let us give thanks to the Lord our God.
All   **It is meet and right so to do.**

It is very meet, right and our bounden duty,
that we should at all times and in all places give thanks unto thee,
O Lord, holy Father,
almighty, everlasting God,
through Jesus Christ thine only Son our Lord.

Short proper preface, when appropriate

[or, when there is no proper preface

For he is the great high priest,
who has loosed us from our sins
and has made us to be a royal priesthood unto thee,
our God and Father.]

Therefore with angels and archangels,
and with all the company of heaven,
we laud and magnify thy glorious name,
evermore praising thee and *saying*:

All   **Holy, holy, holy, Lord God of hosts,**
heaven and earth are full of thy glory.
Glory be to thee, O Lord most high.
[Blessed is he that cometh in the name of the Lord.
Hosanna in the highest.]

sample

All glory be to thee,
almighty God, our heavenly Father,
who, of thy tender mercy,
didst give thine only Son Jesus Christ
to suffer death upon the cross for our redemption;
who made there,
by his one oblation of himself once offered,
a full, perfect and sufficient sacrifice, oblation and satisfaction
    for the sins of the whole world;
and did institute,
and in his holy gospel command us to continue,
a perpetual memory of that his precious death,
until his coming again.

Hear us, O merciful Father, we most humbly beseech thee,
and grant that, by the power of thy Holy Spirit,
we receiving these thy creatures of bread and wine,
according to thy Son our Saviour Jesus Christ's holy institution,
in remembrance of his death and passion,
may be partakers of his most blessed body and blood;

who, in the same night that he was betrayed, took bread;
and when he had given thanks to thee,
he broke it and gave it to his disciples, saying:
Take, eat; this is my body which is given for you;
do this in remembrance of me.

Likewise after supper he took the cup;
and when he had given thanks to thee, he gave it to them, saying:
Drink ye all of this;
for this is my blood of the new covenant,
which is shed for you and for many for the forgiveness of sins.
Do this, as oft as ye shall drink it,
in remembrance of me.

One of the following may be used

[Great is the mystery of faith:]

All **Christ has died:**
Christ is risen:
Christ will come again.

(or)

[Jesus Christ is Lord:]

All **O Saviour of the world,**
who by thy cross and precious blood hast redeemed us,
save us, and help us, we humbly beseech thee, O Lord.

Wherefore, O Lord and heavenly Father,
we thy humble servants,
having in remembrance
the precious death and passion of thy dear Son,
his mighty resurrection and glorious ascension,
entirely desire thy fatherly goodness
mercifully to accept this our sacrifice
of praise and thanksgiving;
most humbly beseeching thee to grant that
by the merits and death of thy Son Jesus Christ,
and through faith in his blood,
we and all thy whole church may obtain
remission of our sins,
and all other benefits of his passion.
And although we be unworthy, through our manifold sins,
to offer unto thee any sacrifice,
yet we beseech thee
to accept this our bounden duty and service,
not weighing our merits, but pardoning our offences;
and to grant that all we, who are partakers of this holy communion,
may be fulfilled with thy grace and heavenly benediction;

through Jesus Christ our Lord,
by whom, and with whom, and in whom,
in the unity of the Holy Spirit,
all honour and glory be unto thee,
O Father almighty,
world without end.

All **Amen.**

The service continues with the Lord's Prayer on page 74.

sample

Let us pray with confidence as our Saviour has taught us

All **Our Father, who art in heaven,
hallowed be thy name;
thy kingdom come;
thy will be done;
on earth as it is in heaven.
Give us this day our daily bread.
And forgive us our trespasses,
as we forgive those who trespass against us.
And lead us not into temptation;
but deliver us from evil.
For thine is the kingdom,
the power and the glory,
for ever and ever.
Amen.**

(or)

As our Saviour taught us, so we pray

All **Our Father in heaven,
hallowed be your name,
your kingdom come,
your will be done,
on earth as in heaven.
Give us today our daily bread.
Forgive us our sins
as we forgive those who sin against us.
Lead us not into temptation
but deliver us from evil.
For the kingdom, the power,
and the glory are yours
now and for ever.
Amen.**

Breaking of the Bread

The president breaks the consecrated bread.

We break this bread
to share in the body of Christ.

All **Though we are many, we are one body,
because we all share in one bread.**

(or)

Every time we eat this bread
and drink this cup,

All **we proclaim the Lord's death
until he comes.**

Agnus Dei may be used as the bread is broken

All **O Lamb of God,
that takest away the sins of the world,
have mercy upon us.**

**O Lamb of God,
that takest away the sins of the world,
have mercy upon us.**

**O Lamb of God,
that takest away the sins of the world,
grant us thy peace.**

sample

Giving of Communion

The president says one of these invitations to communion

Draw near with faith.
Receive the body of our Lord Jesus Christ
which he gave for you,
and his blood which he shed for you.
Eat and drink
in remembrance that he died for you,
and feed on him in your hearts
by faith with thanksgiving.

(or)

Jesus is the Lamb of God
who takes away the sin of the world.
Blessed are those who are called to his supper.

All **Lord, I am not worthy that thou shouldest
come under my roof,
but speak the word only and my soul shall be healed.**

(or)

God's holy gifts
for God's holy people.

All **Jesus Christ is holy,
Jesus Christ is Lord,
to the glory of God the Father.**

or, from Easter Day to Pentecost

Alleluia. Christ our passover is sacrificed for us.

All **Therefore let us keep the feast. Alleluia.**

This prayer may be said before the distribution

All　**We do not presume
to come to this thy table, O merciful Lord,
trusting in our own righteousness,
but in thy manifold and great mercies.
We are not worthy
so much as to gather up the crumbs under thy table.
But thou art the same Lord
whose nature is always to have mercy.
Grant us, therefore, gracious Lord,
so to eat the flesh of thy dear Son Jesus Christ
and to drink his blood,
that our sinful bodies may be made clean by his body
and our souls washed through his most precious blood,
and that we may evermore dwell in him, and he in us.
Amen.**

The president and people receive communion.

Authorized words of distribution are used and the communicant replies

Amen.

During the distribution hymns and anthems may be sung.

If either or both of the consecrated elements are likely to prove insufficient, the president returns to the holy table and adds more, saying the words on page 150.

Any consecrated bread and wine which is not required for purposes of communion is consumed at the end of the distribution or after the service.

sample

Prayer after Communion

Silence is kept.

The post communion, or this or another suitable prayer is said

Almighty and everlasting God, we most heartily thank thee, for that thou dost vouchsafe to feed us, who have duly received these holy mysteries, with the spiritual food of the most precious body and blood of thy Son our Saviour Jesus Christ; and dost assure us thereby of thy favour and goodness towards us; and that we are very members incorporate in the mystical body of thy Son, which is the blessed company of all faithful people, and are also heirs through hope of thy everlasting kingdom, by the merits of the most precious death and passion of thy dear Son. And we most humbly beseech thee, O heavenly Father, so to assist us with thy grace, that we may continue in that holy fellowship, and do all such good works as thou hast prepared for us to walk in; through Jesus Christ our Lord, to whom, with thee and the Holy Spirit, be all honour and glory, world without end.

All **Amen.**

All may say this prayer

All **Almighty God,**
we thank thee for feeding us
with the body and blood of thy Son Jesus Christ.
Through him we offer thee our souls and bodies
to be a living sacrifice.
Send us out
in the power of thy Spirit
to live and work
to thy praise and glory.
Amen.

¶ *The Dismissal*

A hymn may be sung.

The president may use the seasonal blessing, or another suitable blessing

(or)

The peace of God,
which passes all understanding,
keep your hearts and minds
in the knowledge and love of God,
and of his Son Jesus Christ our Lord;
and the blessing of God almighty,
the Father, the Son, and the Holy Spirit,
be among you and remain with you always.

All **Amen.**

A minister says

Go in peace to love and serve the Lord.

All **In the name of Christ. Amen.**

(or)

Go in the peace of Christ.

All **Thanks be to God.**

or, from Easter Day to Pentecost

Go in the peace of Christ. Alleluia, Alleluia.

All **Thanks be to God. Alleluia, Alleluia.**

The ministers and people depart.

sample

Order Two

The people and the priest

¶ prepare for worship

¶ hear and respond to the commandments of God

¶ keep silence and pray a collect

¶ proclaim and respond to the word of God

¶ prepare the table

¶ pray for the Church and the world

¶ confess their sins and are assured of God's forgiveness

¶ praise God for his goodness

¶ pray the Consecration Prayer

¶ receive communion

¶ respond with thanksgiving

¶ depart with God's blessing

For Notes, see pages 184 and 189.

sample

Order Two

A hymn may be sung.

The Lord's Prayer

Our Father, which art in heaven,
hallowed be thy name;
thy kingdom come;
thy will be done;
in earth as it is in heaven.
Give us this day our daily bread.
And forgive us our trespasses,
as we forgive them that trespass against us.
And lead us not into temptation;
but deliver us from evil. Amen.

Prayer of Preparation

Almighty God,
unto whom all hearts be open,
all desires known,
and from whom no secrets are hid:
cleanse the thoughts of our hearts
by the inspiration of thy Holy Spirit,
that we may perfectly love thee,
and worthily magnify thy holy name;
through Christ our Lord.

All **Amen.**

The Commandments

*The priest reads the Ten Commandments and the people make
the response. Or, except on the first Sundays of Advent and Lent,
the Summary of the Law or Kyrie Eleison may be used.*

God spake these words and said:
I am the Lord thy God; thou shalt have none other gods but me.

All **Lord, have mercy upon us,
and incline our hearts to keep this law.**

Thou shalt not make to thyself any graven image,
nor the likeness of any thing that is in heaven above,
or in the earth beneath, or in the water under the earth.
Thou shalt not bow down to them, nor worship them:
for I the Lord thy God am a jealous God,
and visit the sins of the fathers upon the children
    unto the third and fourth generation of them that hate me,
and shew mercy unto thousands in them that love me
    and keep my commandments.

All **Lord, have mercy upon us,
and incline our hearts to keep this law.**

Thou shalt not take the name of the Lord thy God in vain:
for the Lord will not hold him guiltless that taketh his name in vain.

All **Lord, have mercy upon us,
and incline our hearts to keep this law.**

Remember that thou keep holy the Sabbath day.
Six days shalt thou labour, and do all that thou hast to do;
but the seventh day is the Sabbath of the Lord thy God.
In it thou shalt do no manner of work,
thou, and thy son, and thy daughter,
thy manservant, and thy maidservant,
thy cattle, and the stranger that is within thy gates.
For in six days the Lord made heaven and earth,
the sea, and all that in them is,
and rested the seventh day:
wherefore the Lord blessed the seventh day, and hallowed it.

All **Lord, have mercy upon us,
and incline our hearts to keep this law.**

Honour thy father and thy mother;
that thy days may be long in the land
    which the Lord thy God giveth thee.

All   **Lord, have mercy upon us,**
and incline our hearts to keep this law.

Thou shalt do no murder.

All   **Lord, have mercy upon us,**
and incline our hearts to keep this law.

Thou shalt not commit adultery.

All   **Lord, have mercy upon us,**
and incline our hearts to keep this law.

Thou shalt not steal.

All   **Lord, have mercy upon us,**
and incline our hearts to keep this law.

Thou shalt not bear false witness against thy neighbour.

All   **Lord, have mercy upon us,**
and incline our hearts to keep this law.

Thou shalt not covet thy neighbour's house,
thou shalt not covet thy neighbour's wife, nor his servant,
nor his maid, nor his ox, nor his ass, nor anything that is his.

All   **Lord, have mercy upon us,**
and write all these thy laws in our hearts, we beseech thee.

Or this Summary of the Law may be said

Our Lord Jesus Christ said:
Hear, O Israel, the Lord our God is one Lord;
and thou shalt love the Lord thy God with all thy heart,
and with all thy soul, and with all thy mind,
and with all thy strength.
This is the first commandment.

And the second is like, namely this:
Thou shalt love thy neighbour as thyself.
There is none other commandment greater than these.
On these two commandments hang all the law
    and the prophets.

All   **Lord, have mercy upon us, and write all these**
thy laws in our hearts, we beseech thee.

sample

Or Kyrie Eleison may be sung or said

Lord, have mercy.
All **Lord, have mercy.**
Lord, have mercy.

All **Christ, have mercy.**
Christ, have mercy.
All **Christ, have mercy.**

Lord, have mercy.
All **Lord, have mercy.**
Lord, have mercy.

(or)

Kyrie, eleison.
All **Kyrie, eleison**.
Kyrie, eleison.

All **Christe, eleison.**
Christe, eleison.
All **Christe, eleison.**

Kyrie, eleison.
All **Kyrie, eleison**.
Kyrie, eleison.

The Collect for the Sovereign may be said

Almighty God, whose kingdom is everlasting, and power infinite:
Have mercy upon the whole Church; and so rule the heart of
thy chosen servant *Elizabeth*, our Queen and Governor, that she
(knowing whose minister she is) may above all things seek thy
honour and glory: and that we and all her subjects (duly considering
whose authority she hath) may faithfully serve, honour and humbly
obey her, in thee, and for thee, according to thy blessed word and
ordinance; through Jesus Christ our Lord, who with thee and the
Holy Ghost liveth and reigneth, ever one God, world without end.
All **Amen.**

The Collect

The priest may say

The Lord be with you

All **and with thy spirit.**
Let us pray.

The priest says the Collect of the Day.

Epistle

*A Lesson from the Old Testament may be read
and a Psalm may be used.*

The reader says

The Lesson is written in the ... chapter of ...
beginning at the ... verse.

At the end

Here endeth the Lesson.

The reader says

The Epistle is written in the ... chapter of ...
beginning at the ... verse.

At the end

Here endeth the Epistle.

A hymn may be sung.

Gospel

The reader says

The holy Gospel is written in the ... chapter of the Gospel
according to Saint ..., beginning at the ... verse.

All may respond

All **Glory be to thee, O Lord.**

At the end the reader may say

This is the Gospel of the Lord.

All may respond

All **Praise be to thee, O Christ.**

The Creed

*The Creed is used on every Sunday and Holy Day
and may be used on other days also.*

All **I believe in one God the Father almighty,
maker of heaven and earth,
and of all things
visible and invisible:**

**And in one Lord Jesus Christ,
the only-begotten Son of God,
begotten of his Father before all worlds,
God of God, Light of Light,
very God of very God,
begotten, not made,
being of one substance with the Father,
by whom all things were made;
who for us men and for our salvation
came down from heaven,
and was incarnate by the Holy Ghost of the Virgin Mary,
and was made man,
and was crucified also for us under Pontius Pilate.
He suffered and was buried,
and the third day he rose again
according to the Scriptures,
and ascended into heaven,
and sitteth on the right hand of the Father.
And he shall come again with glory
to judge both the quick and the dead:
whose kingdom shall have no end.**

**And I believe in the Holy Ghost,
the Lord and giver of life,
who proceedeth from the Father and the Son,
who with the Father and the Son together
is worshipped and glorified,
who spake by the prophets.
And I believe one catholic and apostolic Church.
I acknowledge one baptism for the remission of sins.
And I look for the resurrection of the dead,
and the life of the world to come.
Amen.**

Banns of marriage may be published and notices given.

Sermon

Offertory

One of the following or another sentence of Scripture is used.

Let your light so shine before men, that they may see your good
works, and glorify your Father which is in heaven.   *Matthew 5.16*

Lay not up for yourselves treasure upon the earth; where the rust
and moth doth corrupt, and where thieves break through and steal:
but lay up for yourselves treasures in heaven; where neither rust
nor moth doth corrupt, and where thieves do not break through
and steal.   *Matthew 6.19*

All things come of thee, and of thine own do we give thee.
1 Chronicles 29.14

Whoso hath this world's good, and seeth his brother have need,
and shutteth up his compassion from him, how dwelleth the love of
God in him?   *1 John 3.17*

A hymn may be sung.

The gifts of the people may be gathered and presented.

The priest places the bread and wine upon the table.

Intercession

Brief biddings may be given.

Let us pray for the whole state of Christ's Church militant here
in earth.

Almighty and ever-living God, who by thy holy apostle hast taught
us to make prayers and supplications, and to give thanks, for all men:
we humbly beseech thee most mercifully *(to accept our alms and
oblations, and)* to receive these our prayers, which we offer unto thy
divine majesty; beseeching thee to inspire continually the universal
Church with the spirit of truth, unity, and concord: and grant, that
all they that do confess thy holy name may agree in the truth of thy
holy word, and live in unity and godly love.

We beseech thee also to save and defend all Christian kings, princes
and governors; and specially thy servant *Elizabeth* our Queen, that
under her we may be godly and quietly governed: and grant unto her
whole Council, and to all that are put in authority under her, that
they may truly and impartially minister justice, to the punishment
of wickedness and vice, and to the maintenance of thy true religion
and virtue.

Give grace, O heavenly Father, to all bishops, priests and deacons,
that they may both by their life and doctrine set forth thy true
and lively word, and rightly and duly administer thy holy sacraments:
and to all thy people give thy heavenly grace; and specially to this
congregation here present; that, with meek heart and due
reverence, they may hear and receive thy holy word; truly serving
thee in holiness and righteousness all the days of their life.

And we most humbly beseech thee of thy goodness, O Lord,
to comfort and succour all them, who in this transitory life are
in trouble, sorrow, need, sickness, or any other adversity.

And we also bless thy holy name for all thy servants departed this
life in thy faith and fear; beseeching thee to give us grace so to
follow their good examples, that with them we may be partakers of
thy heavenly kingdom.

Grant this, O Father, for Jesus Christ's sake, our only mediator
and advocate.

All   **Amen.**

The priest may read the Exhortation (page 99) or one of the other Exhortations in The Book of Common Prayer.

Invitation to Confession

Ye that do truly and earnestly repent you of your sins, and are in love and charity with your neighbours, and intend to lead a new life, following the commandments of God, and walking from henceforth in his holy ways: draw near with faith, and take this holy sacrament to your comfort; and make your humble confession to almighty God, meekly kneeling upon your knees.

Confession

All **Almighty God,**
Father of our Lord Jesus Christ,
maker of all things, judge of all men:
we acknowledge and bewail
    our manifold sins and wickedness,
which we, from time to time,
    most grievously have committed,
by thought, word and deed,
against thy divine majesty,
provoking most justly thy wrath and indignation against us.
We do earnestly repent,
and are heartily sorry for these our misdoings;
the remembrance of them is grievous unto us;
the burden of them is intolerable.
Have mercy upon us,
have mercy upon us, most merciful Father;
for thy Son our Lord Jesus Christ's sake,
forgive us all that is past;
and grant that we may ever hereafter
serve and please thee in newness of life,
to the honour and glory of thy name;
through Jesus Christ our Lord.
Amen.

sample

Absolution

The priest says

Almighty God, our heavenly Father,
who of his great mercy
hath promised forgiveness of sins
to all them that with hearty repentance and true faith
    turn unto him:
have mercy upon *you*;
pardon and deliver *you* from all *your* sins;
confirm and strengthen *you* in all goodness;
and bring *you* to everlasting life;
through Jesus Christ our Lord.

All   **Amen.**

The Comfortable Words

Hear what comfortable words our Saviour Christ saith
unto all that truly turn to him:

Come unto me, all that travail and are heavy laden,
and I will refresh you.   *Matthew 11.28*

God so loved the world, that he gave his only-begotten Son,
to the end that all that believe in him should not perish,
but have everlasting life.   *John 3.16*

Hear also what Saint Paul saith:
This is a true saying, and worthy of all men to be received,
that Christ Jesus came into the world to save sinners.   *1 Timothy 1.15*

Hear also what Saint John saith:
If any man sin, we have an advocate with the Father,
Jesus Christ the righteous;
and he is the propitiation for our sins.   *1 John 2.1-2*

Preface

The priest and the people praise God for his goodness.

The Lord be with you
All   **and with thy spirit.**

Lift up your hearts.
All **We lift them up unto the Lord.**
Let us give thanks unto our Lord God.
All **It is meet and right so to do.**

The priest says

It is very meet, right and our bounden duty,
that we should at all times, and in all places, give thanks unto thee,
O Lord, holy Father,
almighty, everlasting God.

A proper preface may follow (see note 28).

Therefore with angels and archangels,
and with all the company of heaven,
we laud and magnify thy glorious name,
evermore praising thee, and *saying*:

All **Holy, holy, holy, Lord God of hosts,
heaven and earth are full of thy glory.
Glory be to thee, O Lord most high.
(Amen.)**

These words may also be used

All **Blessed is he that cometh in the name of the Lord.
Hosanna in the highest.**

Prayer of Humble Access

We do not presume
to come to this thy table, O merciful Lord,
trusting in our own righteousness,
but in thy manifold and great mercies.
We are not worthy
so much as to gather up the crumbs under thy table.
But thou art the same Lord,
whose property is always to have mercy:
grant us, therefore, gracious Lord,
so to eat the flesh of thy dear Son Jesus Christ,
and to drink his blood,
that our sinful bodies may be made clean by his body,
and our souls washed through his most precious blood,
and that we may evermore dwell in him, and he in us.

All **Amen.**

The Prayer of Consecration

The priest, standing at the table, says the Prayer of Consecration

Almighty God, our heavenly Father, who of thy tender mercy didst
give thine only Son Jesus Christ to suffer death upon the cross for
our redemption; who made there (by his one oblation of himself
once offered) a full, perfect and sufficient sacrifice, oblation and
satisfaction for the sins of the whole world; and did institute, and
in his holy gospel command us to continue, a perpetual memory
of that his precious death, until his coming again:

Hear us, O merciful Father, we most humbly beseech thee;
and grant that we receiving these thy creatures of bread and wine,
according to thy Son our Saviour Jesus Christ's holy institution, in
remembrance of his death and passion, may be partakers of his
most blessed body and blood:

who, in the same night that he was betrayed, took bread;

Here the priest is to take the paten.

and, when he had given thanks, he brake it,

Here the priest shall break the bread.

and gave it to his disciples, saying, Take, eat;

Here the priest is to lay a hand on all the bread.

this is my body which is given for you:
do this in remembrance of me.
Likewise after supper he took the cup;

Here the priest is to take the cup.

and, when he had given thanks, he gave it to them, saying,
Drink ye all of this;

Here the priest is to lay a hand on every vessel
in which there is wine to be consecrated.

for this is my blood of the new testament,
which is shed for you and for many, for the remission of sins:
do this, as oft as ye shall drink it, in remembrance of me.

All **Amen.**

The following may be used

All **O Lamb of God**
that takest away the sins of the world,
have mercy upon us.

O Lamb of God
that takest away the sins of the world,
have mercy upon us.

O Lamb of God
that takest away the sins of the world,
grant us thy peace.

sample

Giving of Communion

The priest and people receive communion. To each is said

The body of our Lord Jesus Christ, which was given for thee,
preserve thy body and soul unto everlasting life.
Take and eat this in remembrance that Christ died for thee,
and feed on him in thy heart by faith with thanksgiving.

The blood of our Lord Jesus Christ, which was shed for thee,
preserve thy body and soul unto everlasting life.
Drink this in remembrance that Christ's blood was shed for thee,
      and be thankful.

*Or, when occasion requires, these words may be said once to each row
of communicants, or to a convenient number within each row.*

*If either or both of the consecrated elements are likely to prove
insufficient, the priest returns to the holy table and adds more,
saying the words on page 150.*

*What remains of the consecrated bread and wine which is not required
for purposes of communion is consumed now or at the end of the service.*

The Lord's Prayer

The priest may say

As our Saviour Christ has commanded and taught us,
we are bold to say

All   **Our Father, which art in heaven,**
hallowed be thy name:
thy kingdom come;
thy will be done;
in earth as it is in heaven.
Give us this day our daily bread.
And forgive us our trespasses,
as we forgive them that trespass against us.
And lead us not into temptation;
but deliver us from evil.
For thine is the kingdom,
the power and the glory,
for ever and ever.
Amen.

Prayer after Communion

The priest says either the Prayer of Oblation or the Prayer of Thanksgiving.

Prayer of Oblation

O Lord and heavenly Father, we thy humble servants entirely desire
thy fatherly goodness mercifully to accept this our sacrifice of praise
and thanksgiving; most humbly beseeching thee to grant, that by
the merits and death of thy Son Jesus Christ, and through faith in
his blood, we and all thy whole Church may obtain remission of our
sins, and all other benefits of his passion. And here we offer and
present unto thee, O Lord, ourselves, our souls and bodies, to be
a reasonable, holy and lively sacrifice unto thee; humbly beseeching
thee, that all we, who are partakers of this holy communion, may
be fulfilled with thy grace and heavenly benediction. And although
we be unworthy, through our manifold sins, to offer unto thee any
sacrifice, yet we beseech thee to accept this our bounden duty
and service; not weighing our merits, but pardoning our offences,
through Jesus Christ our Lord; by whom, and with whom, in the
unity of the Holy Ghost, all honour and glory be unto thee,
O Father almighty, world without end.

All **Amen.**

Prayer of Thanksgiving

Almighty and ever-living God, we most heartily thank thee, for that
thou dost vouchsafe to feed us, who have duly received these holy
mysteries, with the spiritual food of the most precious body and
blood of thy Son our Saviour Jesus Christ; and dost assure us
thereby of thy favour and goodness towards us; and that we are
very members incorporate in the mystical body of thy Son, which
is the blessed company of all faithful people; and are also heirs
through hope of thy everlasting kingdom, by the merits of the most
precious death and passion of thy dear Son. And we most humbly
beseech thee, O heavenly Father, so to assist us with thy grace, that
we may continue in that holy fellowship, and do all such good works
as thou hast prepared for us to walk in; through Jesus Christ our
Lord, to whom, with thee and the Holy Ghost, be all honour and
glory, world without end.

All **Amen.**

Gloria in Excelsis

All   **Glory be to God on high,**
and in earth peace, goodwill towards men.

We praise thee, we bless thee,
we worship thee, we glorify thee,
we give thanks to thee for thy great glory,
O Lord God, heavenly King,
God the Father almighty.

O Lord, the only-begotten Son Jesu Christ;
O Lord God, Lamb of God, Son of the Father,
that takest away the sins of the world,
have mercy upon us.
Thou that takest away the sins of the world,
have mercy upon us.
Thou that takest away the sins of the world,
receive our prayer.
Thou that sittest at the right hand of God the Father,
have mercy upon us.

For thou only art holy;
thou only art the Lord;
thou only, O Christ,
with the Holy Ghost,
art most high
in the glory of God the Father.
Amen.

The Blessing

The priest says

The peace of God, which passeth all understanding, keep your hearts and minds in the knowledge and love of God, and of his Son Jesus Christ our Lord: and the blessing of God almighty, the Father, the Son, and the Holy Ghost, be amongst you and remain with you always.

All   **Amen.**

A hymn may be sung.

¶ Annex to Order Two

Third Exhortation from
The Book of Common Prayer

Dearly beloved in the Lord, ye that mind to come to the holy
Communion of the Body and Blood of our Saviour Christ, must
consider how Saint Paul exhorteth all persons diligently to try
and examine themselves, before they presume to eat of that Bread,
and drink of that Cup. For as the benefit is great, if with a true
penitent heart and lively faith we receive that holy Sacrament;
(for then we spiritually eat the flesh of Christ and drink his blood;
then we dwell in Christ, and Christ in us; we are one with Christ,
and Christ with us;) so is the danger great, if we receive the same
unworthily. For then we are guilty of the Body and Blood of Christ
our Saviour; we eat and drink our own damnation, not considering
the Lord's Body; we kindle God's wrath against us; we provoke him
to plague us with divers diseases, and sundry kinds of death. Judge
therefore yourselves, brethren, that ye be not judged of the Lord;
repent you truly for your sins past; have a lively and steadfast faith
in Christ our Saviour; amend your lives, and be in perfect charity
with all men; so shall ye be meet partakers of those holy mysteries.
And above all things ye must give most humble and hearty thanks
to God, the Father, the Son and the Holy Ghost, for the redemption
of the world by the death and passion of our Saviour Christ, both
God and man; who did humble himself, even to the death upon the
Cross, for us miserable sinners, who lay in darkness and the shadow
of death; that he might make us the children of God, and exalt us
to everlasting life. And to the end that we should always remember
the exceeding great love of our Master and only Saviour Jesus Christ,
thus dying for us, and the innumerable benefits which by his precious
blood-shedding he hath obtained to us; he hath instituted and
ordained holy mysteries, as pledges of his love, and for a continual
remembrance of his death, to our great and endless comfort. To him,
therefore, with the Father and the Holy Ghost, let us give (as we are
most bounden) continual thanks; submitting ourselves wholly to his
holy will and pleasure, and studying to serve him in true holiness
and righteousness all the days of our life.

All **Amen.**

sample

Proper Prefaces from
The Book of Common Prayer

For additional prefaces, see note 28 and texts on pages 154–83.

Christmas

Because thou didst give Jesus Christ thine only Son to be born
as at this time for us; who, by the operation of the Holy Ghost,
was made very man of the substance of the Virgin Mary his mother;
and that without spot of sin, to make us clean from all sin.
Therefore with angels …

Easter

But chiefly are we bound to praise thee for the glorious resurrection
of thy Son Jesus Christ our Lord: for he is the very paschal lamb,
which was offered for us, and hath taken away the sin of the world;
who by his death hath destroyed death, and by his rising to life again
hath restored to us everlasting life.
Therefore with angels …

Ascension

Through thy most dearly beloved Son Jesus Christ our Lord;
who after his most glorious resurrection manifestly appeared to all
his apostles, and in their sight ascended up into heaven to prepare
a place for us; that where he is, thither we might also ascend, and
reign with him in glory.
Therefore with angels …

Pentecost (Whitsun)

Through Jesus Christ our Lord; according to whose most true
promise, the Holy Ghost came down as at this time from heaven
with a sudden great sound, as it might have been a mighty wind,
in the likeness of fiery tongues, lighting upon the apostles, to teach
them, and to lead them to all truth; giving them both the gift of
divers languages, and also boldness with fervent zeal constantly to
preach the gospel unto all nations; whereby we have been brought
out of darkness and error into the clear light and true knowledge
of thee, and of thy Son Jesus Christ.
Therefore with angels …

Trinity Sunday

Who art one God, one Lord; not one only Person, but three Persons
in one Substance. For that which we believe of the glory of the
Father, the same we believe of the Son, and of the Holy Ghost,
without any difference or inequality.
Therefore with angels …

sample

Order Two *in Contemporary Language*

A hymn may be sung.

The Lord's Prayer may be said.

Prayer of Preparation

Almighty God,
to whom all hearts are open,
all desires known,
and from whom no secrets are hidden:
cleanse the thoughts of our hearts
by the inspiration of your Holy Spirit,
that we may perfectly love you,
and worthily magnify your holy name;
through Christ our Lord.

All　**Amen.**

sample

The Commandments

The president reads the Ten Commandments and the people make the response. Or, except on the first Sundays of Advent and Lent, the Summary of the Law (page 122) or Kyrie Eleison may be used. At the discretion of the minister, responses may be used only after the fourth and tenth Commandments, or only after the tenth Commandment.

I am the Lord your God [who brought you out of the land of Egypt, out of the house of slavery]; you shall have no other gods but me.

All **Lord, have mercy upon us,**
and incline our hearts to keep this law.

You shall not make for yourself an idol,
whether in the form of anything that is in heaven above,
or that is on the earth beneath, or that is in the water
    under the earth.
You shall not bow down to them or worship them.
[For I the Lord your God am a jealous God,
punishing children for the iniquity of parents
to the third and the fourth generation of those who reject me,
but showing steadfast love to a thousand generations of those
    who love me
and keep my commandments.]

All **Lord, have mercy upon us,**
and incline our hearts to keep this law.

You shall not take the name of the Lord your God in vain
[for the Lord will not hold him guiltless who takes his name in vain].

All **Lord, have mercy upon us,**
and incline our hearts to keep this law.

Remember the Sabbath day, and keep it holy.
For six days you shall labour and do all your work.
But the seventh day is a Sabbath to the Lord your God.
[You shall not do any work –
you, your son or your daughter,
your slaves, your livestock,
or the foreigner who lives among you.
For in six days the Lord made heaven and earth,
the sea, and all that is in them,
but rested the seventh day;
therefore the Lord blessed the seventh day and consecrated it.]

All **Lord, have mercy upon us,**
and incline our hearts to keep this law.

Honour your father and your mother
[so that your days may be long in the land
that the Lord your God is giving you].

All **Lord, have mercy upon us,
and incline our hearts to keep this law.**

You shall not murder.

All **Lord, have mercy upon us,
and incline our hearts to keep this law.**

You shall not commit adultery.

All **Lord, have mercy upon us,
and incline our hearts to keep this law.**

You shall not steal.

All **Lord, have mercy upon us,
and incline our hearts to keep this law.**

You shall not bear false witness [against your neighbour].

All **Lord, have mercy upon us,
and incline our hearts to keep this law.**

You shall not covet [your neighbour's house;
you shall not covet your neighbour's wife, or slaves, or ox, or donkey,
or anything that belongs to your neighbour].

All **Lord, have mercy upon us,
and write all these your laws in our hearts.**

The Collect for the Sovereign may be said.

Almighty God,
the fountain of all goodness,
bless our Sovereign Lady, Queen *Elizabeth,*
and all who are in authority under her;
that they may order all things
    in wisdom and equity, righteousness and peace,
to the honour and glory of your name
and the good of your Church and people;
through Jesus Christ your Son our Lord,
who is alive and reigns with you,
in the unity of the Holy Spirit,
one God, now and for ever.

All **Amen.**

sample

The Collect

*The president introduces a period of silent prayer with the words
'Let us pray' or a more specific bidding.*

The Collect is said, and all respond

All **Amen.**

Readings

Either one or two readings from Scripture precede the Gospel reading.

At the end of each the reader may say

This is the word of the Lord.
All **Thanks be to God.**

*The psalm or canticle follows the first reading, and other hymns
and songs may be used between the readings.*

Gospel Reading

An acclamation may herald the Gospel reading.

When the Gospel is announced the reader says

Hear the Gospel of our Lord Jesus Christ according to N.
All **Glory to you, O Lord.**

At the end the reader may say

This is the Gospel of the Lord.
All **Praise to you, O Christ.**

The Creed

On Sundays and principal holy days an authorized translation of the Nicene Creed is used, or on occasion the Apostles' Creed or an authorized affirmation of faith may be used (see pages 00–00).

All **We believe in one God,**
the Father, the almighty,
maker of heaven and earth,
of all that is,
seen and unseen.

We believe in one Lord, Jesus Christ,
the only Son of God,
eternally begotten of the Father,
God from God, Light from Light,
true God from true God,
begotten, not made,
of one Being with the Father;
through him all things were made.
For us and for our salvation he came down from heaven,
he became incarnate from the Holy Spirit and the Virgin Mary
and was made man.
For our sake he was crucified under Pontius Pilate;
he suffered death and was buried.
On the third day he rose again
in accordance with the Scriptures;
he ascended into heaven
and is seated at the right hand of the Father.
He will come again in glory to judge the living and the dead,
and his kingdom will have no end.

We believe in the Holy Spirit,
the Lord, the giver of life,
who proceeds from the Father and the Son,
who with the Father and the Son is worshipped and glorified,
who has spoken through the prophets.
We believe in one holy catholic and apostolic Church.
We acknowledge one baptism for the forgiveness of sins.
We look for the resurrection of the dead,
and the life of the world to come.
Amen.

sample

Sermon

Offertory

One of the following or another sentence of Scripture is used.

Let your light shine before others, so that they may see your good works, and give glory to your Father in heaven.   *Matthew 5.16*

Do not store up for yourselves treasures on earth; where moth and rust consume, and where thieves break in and steal: but store up for yourselves treasures in heaven, where neither rust nor moth consume, and where thieves do not break in and steal.

Matthew 6.19

All things come from you, and of your own have we given you.

1 Chronicles 29.14

How does God's love abide in anyone who has the world's goods and sees a brother or sister in need and yet refuses help?

1 John 3.17

A hymn may be sung.

The gifts of the people may be gathered and presented.

The president places the bread and wine on the table.

Prayers of Intercession

One of the forms on pages 135–41 or other suitable words may be used.

The prayers usually include these concerns and may follow this sequence:

¶ *The Church of Christ*

¶ *Creation, human society, the Sovereign and those in authority*

¶ *The local community*

¶ *Those who suffer*

¶ *The communion of saints*

These responses may be used

Lord, in your mercy
All **hear our prayer.**

(or)

Lord, hear us.
All **Lord, graciously hear us.**

And at the end

Merciful Father,
All **accept these prayers
for the sake of your Son,
our Saviour Jesus Christ.
Amen.**

sample

Prayers of Penitence

A minister reads this shorter exhortation

Brothers and sisters in Christ,
as we gather at the Lord's table
we must recall the promises and warnings
    given to us in the Scriptures.
Let us therefore examine ourselves and repent of our sins.
Let us give thanks to God
    for his redemption of the world through his Son Jesus Christ,
and as we remember Christ's death for us,
and receive this pledge of his love,
let us resolve to serve him in holiness and righteousness
all the days of our life.

Invitation to Confession

*A minister uses a seasonal invitation to confession or these
or other suitable words*

You then, who truly and earnestly repent of your sins,
and are in love and charity with your neighbours,
and intend to lead a new life,
following the commandments of God,
and walking from this day forward in his holy ways:
draw near with faith,
and take this holy sacrament to your comfort;
and make your humble confession to almighty God.

Confession

Either of these forms, or form 2 on page 130 may be used.

All   **Almighty God,**
Father of our Lord Jesus Christ,
maker of all things, judge of all people,
we acknowledge and lament our many sins
and the wickedness we have committed time after time,
by thought, word and deed against your divine majesty.
We have provoked your righteous anger
and your indignation against us.
We earnestly repent,
and are deeply sorry for these our wrongdoings;
the memory of them weighs us down,
the burden of them is too great for us to bear.
Have mercy upon us,
have mercy upon us, most merciful Father.
For your Son our Lord Jesus Christ's sake,
forgive us all that is past;
and grant that from this time forward
we may always serve and please you in newness of life,
to the honour and glory of your name;
through Jesus Christ our Lord.
Amen.

(or)

All   **Father eternal, giver of light and grace,**
we have sinned against you and against our neighbour,
in what we have thought,
in what we have said and done,
through ignorance, through weakness,
through our own deliberate fault.
We have wounded your love,
and marred your image in us.
We are sorry and ashamed,
and repent of all our sins.
For the sake of your Son Jesus Christ,
who died for us,
forgive us all that is past;
and lead us out from darkness
to walk as children of light.
Amen.

sample

Absolution

The president says

Almighty God, our heavenly Father,
who in his great mercy
has promised forgiveness of sins
to all those who with heartfelt repentance and true faith
    turn to him:
have mercy on *you*,
pardon and deliver *you* from all *your* sins,
confirm and strengthen *you* in all goodness,
and bring *you* to everlasting life,
through Jesus Christ our Lord.

All **Amen.**

The Comfortable Words

Hear the words of comfort our Saviour Christ says
to all who truly turn to him:

Come to me, all who labour and are heavy laden,
and I will give you rest. *Matthew 11.28*

God so loved the world that he gave his only-begotten Son,
that whoever believes in him should not perish
but have eternal life. *John 3.16*

Hear what Saint Paul says:
This saying is true and worthy of full acceptance,
that Christ Jesus came into the world to save sinners. *1 Timothy 1.15*

Hear what Saint John says:
If anyone sins, we have an advocate with the Father,
Jesus Christ the righteous;
and he is the propitiation for our sins. *1 John 2.1-2*

Preface

The president and the people praise God for his goodness.

Lift up your hearts.
All **We lift them to the Lord.**

Let us give thanks to the Lord our God.
All **It is right to give thanks and praise.**

It is indeed right,
it is our duty and our joy,
at all times and in all places
to give you thanks and praise,
holy Father, heavenly King,
almighty and eternal God.

A proper preface may follow (see note 28).

Therefore with angels and archangels,
and with all the company of heaven,
we proclaim your great and glorious name,
for ever praising you, and *saying*:

All **Holy, holy, holy Lord,**
God of power and might,
heaven and earth are full of your glory.
Hosanna in the highest.

sample

Prayer of Humble Access

One of these prayers is said.

We do not presume
to come to this your table, merciful Lord,
trusting in our own righteousness,
but in your manifold and great mercies.
We are not worthy
so much as to gather up the crumbs under your table.
But you are the same Lord
whose nature is always to have mercy.
Grant us therefore, gracious Lord,
so to eat the flesh of your dear Son Jesus Christ
and to drink his blood,
that our sinful bodies may be made clean by his body,
and our souls washed through his most precious blood,
and that we may evermore dwell in him, and he in us.

All **Amen.**

(or)

Most merciful Lord,
your love compels us to come in.
Our hands were unclean,
our hearts were unprepared;
we were not fit
even to eat the crumbs from under your table.
But you, Lord, are the God of our salvation,
and share your bread with sinners.
So cleanse and feed us
with the precious body and blood of your Son,
that he may live in us and we in him;
and that we, with the whole company of Christ,
may sit and eat in your kingdom.

All **Amen**.

The Prayer of Consecration

The president, standing at the table, says the Prayer of Consecration.

Almighty God, our heavenly Father,
who, in your tender mercy,
gave your only Son our Saviour Jesus Christ
to suffer death upon the cross for our redemption;
who made there by his one oblation of himself once offered
a full, perfect and sufficient sacrifice, oblation and satisfaction
    for the sins of the whole world;
he instituted, and in his holy gospel commanded us to continue,
a perpetual memory of his precious death until he comes again.

Hear us, merciful Father, we humbly pray,
and grant that we receiving these gifts of your creation,
    this bread and this wine,
according to your Son our Saviour Jesus Christ's holy institution,
in remembrance of his death and passion,
may be partakers of his most blessed body and blood;

who, in the same night that he was betrayed,
took bread and gave you thanks,
> *Here the president takes the paten.*

he broke it and gave it to his disciples, saying:
> *Here the president breaks the bread.*

Take, eat, this is my body which is given for you;
> *Here the president lays a hand on all the bread.*

do this in remembrance of me.
In the same way, after supper, he took the cup;
> *Here the president takes the cup.*

and when he had given thanks, he gave it to them, saying:
Drink this, all of you, this is my blood of the new covenant,
which is shed for you and for many
for the forgiveness of sins.
> *Here the president is to lay a hand on every vessel*
> *in which there is wine to be consecrated.*

Do this, as often as you drink it,
in remembrance of me.

All **Amen.**

sample

Giving of Communion

The president and people receive communion.

To each is said

The body of our Lord Jesus Christ,
which was given for you,
preserve your body and soul to everlasting life.
Take and eat this in remembrance that Christ died for you,
and feed on him in your heart by faith with thanksgiving.

The blood of our Lord Jesus Christ,
which was shed for you,
preserve your body and soul to everlasting life.
Drink this in remembrance that Christ's blood was shed for you,
    and be thankful.

*Or, when occasion requires, these words may be said once to each row
of communicants, or to a convenient number within each row.*

*If either or both of the consecrated elements are likely to prove
insufficient, the president returns to the holy table and adds more, saying
the words on page 150.*

*What remains of the consecrated bread and wine which is not required
for purposes of communion is consumed now or at the end of the
service.*

The Lord's Prayer

The Lord's Prayer is said.

As our Saviour taught us, so we pray

All **Our Father in heaven,**
hallowed be your name,
your kingdom come,
your will be done,
on earth as in heaven.
Give us today our daily bread.
Forgive us our sins
as we forgive those who sin against us.
Lead us not into temptation
but deliver us from evil.
For the kingdom, the power,
and the glory are yours
now and for ever.
Amen.

(or)

Let us pray with confidence as our Saviour has taught us

All **Our Father, who art in heaven,**
hallowed be thy name;
thy kingdom come;
thy will be done;
on earth as it is in heaven.
Give us this day our daily bread.
And forgive us our trespasses,
as we forgive those who trespass against us.
And lead us not into temptation;
but deliver us from evil.
For thine is the kingdom,
the power and the glory,
for ever and ever.
Amen.

sample

Prayer after Communion

The president says one of the following prayers or the prayer on page 152.

Lord and heavenly Father,
we offer you through your dear Son Jesus Christ
    this our sacrifice of praise and thanksgiving.
Grant that by his merits and death,
and through faith in his blood,
we and all your Church may receive forgiveness of our sins
and all other benefits of his passion.

And here we offer and present to you, O Lord,
    ourselves, our souls and our bodies,
to be a reasonable, holy and living sacrifice;
fill us all who share in this holy communion
with your grace and heavenly blessing.

Although we are unworthy, through our manifold sins,
to offer you any sacrifice,
yet we pray that you will accept this
the duty and service that we owe.
Do not weigh our merits, but pardon our offences,
through Jesus Christ our Lord,
by whom, and with whom, and in whom,
in the unity of the Holy Spirit,
all honour and glory be yours, almighty Father,
for ever and ever.

All **Amen.**

(or)

Father of all,
we give you thanks and praise,
that when we were still far off
you met us in your Son and brought us home.
Dying and living, he declared your love,
gave us grace, and opened the gate of glory.
May we who share Christ's body live his risen life;
we who drink his cup bring life to others;
we whom the Spirit lights give light to the world.
Keep us firm in the hope you have set before us,
so we and all your children shall be free,
and the whole earth live to praise your name;
through Christ our Lord.

All   **Amen.**

Gloria in Excelsis

All   **Glory to God in the highest,**
and peace to his people on earth.

Lord God, heavenly King,
almighty God and Father,
we worship you, we give you thanks,
we praise you for your glory.

Lord Jesus Christ, only Son of the Father,
Lord God, Lamb of God,
you take away the sin of the world:
have mercy on us;
you are seated at the right hand of the Father:
receive our prayer.

For you alone are the Holy One,
you alone are the Lord,
you alone are the Most High, Jesus Christ,
with the Holy Spirit,
in the glory of God the Father.
Amen.

Or another song of praise may be used.

The Blessing

The president may use a seasonal blessing
or another suitable blessing, or

The peace of God,
which passes all understanding,
keep your hearts and minds
in the knowledge and love of God,
and of his Son Jesus Christ our Lord;
and the blessing of God almighty,
the Father, the Son, and the Holy Spirit,
be among you, and remain with you always.

All **Amen.**

A hymn may be sung.

Supplementary Texts

¶ *Penitential Material*

Summary of the Law

This may be used with or without the congregational response.

Our Lord Jesus Christ said:
The first commandment is this:
'Hear, O Israel, the Lord our God is the only Lord.
You shall love the Lord your God with all your heart,
with all your soul, with all your mind,
and with all your strength.'

The second is this: 'Love your neighbour as yourself.'
There is no other commandment greater than these.
On these two commandments hang all the law and the prophets.

All **Amen. Lord, have mercy.**

(or)

Our Lord Jesus Christ said:
Hear, O Israel, the Lord our God is one Lord;
and thou shalt love the Lord thy God with all thy heart,
and with all thy soul, and with all thy mind,
and with all thy strength.
This is the first commandment.

And the second is like, namely this:
Thou shalt love thy neighbour as thyself.
There is none other commandment greater than these.
On these two commandments hang all the law and the prophets.

All **Lord, have mercy upon us, and write all these thy laws
in our hearts, we beseech thee.**

The Commandments

I

Hear these commandments which God has given to his people
and examine your hearts.

God spake these words and said:
I am the Lord thy God; thou shalt have none other gods but me.

All **Lord, have mercy upon us,**
and incline our hearts to keep this law.

Thou shalt not make to thyself any graven image,
nor the likeness of any thing that is in heaven above,
or in the earth beneath, or in the water under the earth.
Thou shalt not bow down to them, nor worship them.
[For I the Lord thy God am a jealous God,
and visit the sins of the fathers upon the children
   unto the third and fourth generation of them that hate me,
and shew mercy unto thousands in them that love me
   and keep my commandments.]

All **Lord, have mercy upon us,**
and incline our hearts to keep this law.

Thou shalt not take the name of the Lord thy God in vain
[for the Lord will not hold him guiltless that taketh his name in vain].

All **Lord, have mercy upon us,**
and incline our hearts to keep this law.

Remember that thou keep holy the Sabbath day.
Six days shalt thou labour, and do all that thou hast to do;
but the seventh day is the Sabbath of the Lord thy God.
[In it thou shalt do no manner of work,
thou, and thy son, and thy daughter,
thy manservant, and thy maidservant,
thy cattle, and the stranger that is within thy gates.
For in six days the Lord made heaven and earth,
the sea, and all that in them is,
and rested the seventh day:
wherefore the Lord blessed the seventh day, and hallowed it.]

All **Lord, have mercy upon us,**
and incline our hearts to keep this law.

sample

Honour thy father and thy mother
[that thy days may be long in the land
which the Lord thy God giveth thee].

All   **Lord, have mercy upon us,
and incline our hearts to keep this law.**

Thou shalt do no murder.

All   **Lord, have mercy upon us,
and incline our hearts to keep this law.**

Thou shalt not commit adultery.

All   **Lord, have mercy upon us,
and incline our hearts to keep this law.**

Thou shalt not steal.

All   **Lord, have mercy upon us,
and incline our hearts to keep this law.**

Thou shalt not bear false witness [against thy neighbour].

All   **Lord, have mercy upon us,
and incline our hearts to keep this law.**

Thou shalt not covet [thy neighbour's house,
thou shalt not covet thy neighbour's wife, nor his servant,
nor his maid, nor his ox, nor his ass, nor anything that is his].

All   **Lord, have mercy upon us, and write all these thy laws
in our hearts, we beseech thee.**

2

Hear these commandments which God has given to his people,
and examine your hearts.

I am the Lord your God: you shall have no other gods but me.
You shall love the Lord your God with all your heart,
with all your soul, with all your mind, and with all your strength.

All   **Amen. Lord, have mercy.**

You shall not make for yourself any idol.
God is spirit, and those who worship him must worship in spirit
and in truth.

All   **Amen. Lord, have mercy.**

You shall not dishonour the name of the Lord your God.
You shall worship him with awe and reverence.

All **Amen. Lord, have mercy.**

Remember the Sabbath and keep it holy.
Christ is risen from the dead: set your minds on things that are
above, not on things that are on the earth.

All **Amen. Lord, have mercy.**

Honour your father and mother.
Live as servants of God; let us work for the good of all,
especially members of the household of faith.

All **Amen. Lord, have mercy.**

You shall not commit murder.
Live peaceably with all; overcome evil with good.

All **Amen. Lord, have mercy.**

You shall not commit adultery.
Know that your body is a temple of the Holy Spirit.

All **Amen. Lord, have mercy.**

You shall not steal.
Be honest in all that you do, and care for those in need.

All **Amen. Lord, have mercy.**

You shall not be a false witness.
Let everyone speak the truth.

All **Amen. Lord, have mercy.**

You shall not covet anything which belongs to your neighbour.
Remember the words of the Lord Jesus:
'It is more blessed to give than to receive.'
Love your neighbour as yourself, for love is the fulfilling of the law.

All **Amen. Lord, have mercy.**

The Beatitudes

Silence is kept between each Beatitude.

Let us hear our Lord's blessing on those who follow him.

Blessed are the poor in spirit,
for theirs is the kingdom of heaven.

Blessed are those who mourn,
for they shall be comforted.

Blessed are the meek,
for they shall inherit the earth.

Blessed are those who hunger and thirst after righteousness,
for they shall be satisfied.

Blessed are the merciful,
for they shall obtain mercy.

Blessed are the pure in heart,
for they shall see God.

Blessed are the peacemakers,
for they shall be called children of God.

Blessed are those who suffer persecution for righteousness' sake,
for theirs is the kingdom of heaven.

Let us confess our many failures to keep this way of truth and life.

The confession follows without further invitation.

The Comfortable Words

One or more of these sentences may be used

Hear the words of comfort our Saviour Christ says
to all who truly turn to him:

Come to me, all who labour and are heavy laden,
and I will give you rest. *Matthew 11.28*

God so loved the world that he gave his only-begotten Son,
that whoever believes in him should not perish
but have eternal life. *John 3.16*

Hear what Saint Paul says:
This saying is true, and worthy of full acceptance,
that Christ Jesus came into the world to save sinners. *1 Timothy 1.15*

Hear what Saint John says:
If anyone sins, we have an advocate with the Father,
Jesus Christ the righteous;
and he is the propitiation for our sins. *1 John 2.1-2*

(Let us confess our sins in penitence and faith.)

(or)

Hear what comfortable words our Saviour Christ saith
unto all that truly turn to him:

Come unto me, all that travail and are heavy laden,
and I will refresh you. *Matthew 11.28*

God so loved the world, that he gave his only-begotten Son,
to the end that all that believe in him should not perish,
but have everlasting life. *John 3.16*

Hear what Saint Paul saith:
This is a true saying, and worthy of all men to be received,
that Christ Jesus came into the world to save sinners. *1 Timothy 1.15*

Hear what Saint John saith:
If any man sin, we have an advocate with the Father,
Jesus Christ the righteous;
and he is the propitiation for our sins. *1 John 2.1-2*

(Let us confess our sins in penitence and faith.)

Exhortation

Brothers and sisters in Christ,
as we gather at the Lord's table
we must recall the promises and warnings
    given to us in the Scriptures.
Let us therefore examine ourselves and repent of our sins.
Let us give thanks to God
    for his redemption of the world through his Son Jesus Christ,
and as we remember Christ's death for us,
and receive this pledge of his love,
let us resolve to serve him in holiness and righteousness
all the days of our life.

Invitations to Confession

The provision made for seasons and principal holy days
(see pages 154–83) may be used at other times when appropriate.

1

My brothers and sisters,
as we prepare to celebrate the presence of Christ
in word and sacrament,
let us call to mind and confess our sins.

2

Jesus said:
Before you offer your gift,
go and be reconciled.
As brothers and sisters in God's family,
we come together to ask our Father for forgiveness.

3

Ye that do truly and earnestly repent you of your sins,
and are in love and charity with your neighbours,
and intend to lead a new life,
following the commandments of God,
and walking from henceforth in his holy ways:
draw near with faith,
and take this holy sacrament to your comfort;
and make your humble confession to almighty God.

4

This invitation may be used after the Commandments,
the Comfortable Words or the Exhortation, or may be introduced
by a penitential sentence of Scripture

You then, who truly and earnestly repent of your sins,
and are in love and charity with your neighbours,
and intend to lead a new life,
following the commandments of God
and walking from henceforth in his holy ways:
draw near with faith,
and take this holy sacrament to your comfort;
and make your humble confession to almighty God.

The confession follows without further invitation.

sample

For other authorized confessions, see page 00.

1

All   **Father eternal, giver of light and grace,
we have sinned against you and against our neighbour,
in what we have thought,
in what we have said and done,
through ignorance, through weakness,
through our own deliberate fault.
We have wounded your love,
and marred your image in us.
We are sorry and ashamed,
and repent of all our sins.
For the sake of your Son Jesus Christ,
who died for us,
forgive us all that is past;
and lead us out from darkness
to walk as children of light.
Amen.**

2

All   **Almighty God, our heavenly Father,
we have sinned against you,
through our own fault,
in thought, and word, and deed,
and in what we have left undone.
We are heartily sorry,
and repent of all our sins.
For your Son our Lord Jesus Christ's sake,
forgive us all that is past;
and grant that we may serve you in newness of life
to the glory of your name.
Amen.**

3

All   **Almighty God,**
Father of our Lord Jesus Christ,
maker of all things, judge of all men:
we acknowledge and bewail
    our manifold sins and wickedness,
which we, from time to time,
    most grievously have committed,
by thought, word and deed,
against thy divine majesty,
provoking most justly thy wrath and indignation against us.
We do earnestly repent,
and are heartily sorry for these our misdoings;
the remembrance of them is grievous unto us;
the burden of them is intolerable.
Have mercy upon us,
have mercy upon us, most merciful Father;
for thy Son our Lord Jesus Christ's sake,
forgive us all that is past;
and grant that we may ever hereafter
serve and please thee in newness of life,
to the honour and glory of thy name;
through Jesus Christ our Lord.
Amen.

4

Wash me thoroughly from my wickedness
and cleanse me from my sin.
Lord, have mercy.

All   **Lord, have mercy.**

Make me a clean heart, O God,
and renew a right spirit within me.
Christ, have mercy.

All   **Christ, have mercy.**

Cast me not away from your presence
and take not your holy spirit from me.
Lord, have mercy.

All   **Lord, have mercy.**

5

In the wilderness we find your grace;
you love us with an everlasting love.
Lord, have mercy.

All **Lord, have mercy.**

There is none but you to uphold our cause;
our sin cries out and our guilt is great.
Christ, have mercy.

All **Christ, have mercy.**

Heal us, O Lord, and we shall be healed;
restore us and we shall know your joy.
Lord, have mercy.

All **Lord, have mercy.**

6

Remember, Lord, your compassion and love,
for they are everlasting.
Lord, have mercy.

All **Lord, have mercy.**

Remember not the sins of my youth or my transgressions,
but think on me in your goodness, O Lord,
    according to your steadfast love.
Christ, have mercy.

All **Christ, have mercy.**

O keep my soul and deliver me;
let me not be put to shame, for I have put my trust in you.
Lord, have mercy.

All **Lord, have mercy.**

Absolutions

For other authorized absolutions, see page 00.

1
Almighty God, our heavenly Father,
who of his great mercy
hath promised forgiveness of sins
to all them that with hearty repentance and true faith
    turn unto him:
have mercy upon *you*;
pardon and deliver *you* from all *your* sins;
confirm and strengthen *you* in all goodness;
and bring *you* to everlasting life;
through Jesus Christ our Lord.

All **Amen.**

2
May almighty God have mercy on *you*,
forgive *you your* sins,
and bring *you* to everlasting life.

All **Amen.**

¶ Gospel Acclamations for Ordinary Time

1

Alleluia, alleluia.

Speak, Lord, for your servant is listening.

You have the words of eternal life.   *1 Samuel 3.9; John 6.68*

All   **Alleluia.**

2

Alleluia, alleluia.

I am the light of the world, says the Lord.

Whoever follows me will never walk in darkness

but will have the light of life.   *John 8.12*

All   **Alleluia.**

3

Alleluia, alleluia.

My sheep hear my voice, says the Lord.

I know them, and they follow me.   *John 10.27*

All   **Alleluia.**

4

Alleluia, alleluia.

I am the way, the truth, and the life, says the Lord.

No one comes to the Father except through me.   *John 14.6*

All   **Alleluia.**

5

Alleluia, alleluia.

We do not live by bread alone,

but by every word that comes from the mouth of God.   *Matthew 4.4*

All   **Alleluia.**

6

Alleluia, alleluia.

Welcome with meekness the implanted word

that has the power to save your souls.   *James 1.21*

All   **Alleluia.**

7

Alleluia, alleluia.

The word of the Lord endures for ever.

The word of the Lord is the good news announced to you.

All   **Alleluia.**   *cf 1 Peter 1.25*

¶ Forms of Intercession

1

This form may be used either with the insertion of specific subjects between the paragraphs or as a continuous whole, with or without brief biddings addressed to the people before the prayer begins.

Not all paragraphs need to be used on every occasion.

Individual names may be added at the places indicated.

The responses indicated in the service order may be used at appropriate points in the text.

At the end of this form of intercession, silence may be kept and a collect or other ending may be said (see page 142).

In the power of the Spirit and in union with Christ,
let us pray to the Father.

Almighty God, our heavenly Father,
you promised through your Son Jesus Christ
to hear us when we pray in faith.

Strengthen *N* our bishop and all your Church in the service of Christ,
that those who confess your name may be united in your truth,
live together in your love, and reveal your glory in the world.

Bless and guide *Elizabeth* our Queen; give wisdom to all in authority;
and direct this and every nation in the ways of justice and of peace;
that we may honour one another, and seek the common good.

Give grace to us, our families and friends, and to all our neighbours,
that we may serve Christ in one another, and love as he loves us.

Comfort and heal all those who suffer in body, mind, or spirit ...;
give them courage and hope in their troubles;
and bring them the joy of your salvation.

Hear us as we remember those who have died in the faith of Christ ...;
according to your promises,
grant us with them a share in your eternal kingdom.

Rejoicing in the fellowship of *(N and of)* all your saints,
we commend ourselves and the whole creation to your unfailing love.

Silence may be kept and a collect or other ending may be said.

sample

2

*This form may be used either with the insertion of specific subjects
at the points indicated or as a continuous whole, with or without
brief biddings addressed to the people before the prayer begins.*

*The responses indicated in the service order may be used
at appropriate points in the text.*

In the power of the Spirit and in union with Christ,
let us pray to the Father.

O God, the creator and preserver of all,
we pray for people in every kind of need;
make your ways known on earth,
your saving health among all nations ...

We pray for the good estate of the catholic Church;
guide and govern us by your good Spirit,
that all who profess and call themselves Christians
may be led into the way of truth,
and hold the faith in unity of spirit,
in the bond of peace and in righteousness of life ...

We commend to your fatherly goodness
all those who are any ways afflicted or distressed,
in mind, body or estate;
comfort and relieve them in their need,
give them patience in their sufferings,
and bring good out of all their afflictions ...

We remember those who have gone before us
in the peace of Christ,
and we give you praise for all your faithful ones,
with whom we rejoice in the communion of saints ...

All this we ask for Jesus Christ's sake.

All **Amen.**

3

This form is used as a continuous whole without interpolation
except, if desired, the inclusion of responses printed in the service order.
However, biddings may be addressed to the people before the prayer
begins. Not all paragraphs need be used on every occasion.

In the power of the Spirit and in union with Christ, let us pray to
the Father.

Almighty and ever-living God, who by thy holy apostle hast taught
us to make prayers and supplications, and to give thanks, for all
men: we humbly beseech thee most mercifully to receive these our
prayers, which we offer unto thy divine majesty; beseeching thee
to inspire continually the universal Church with the spirit of truth,
unity and concord; and grant that all they that do confess thy holy
name may agree in the truth of thy holy word, and live in unity and
godly love.

We beseech thee also to lead all nations in the way of righteousness
and peace; and so to direct all kings and rulers, that under them
thy people may be godly and quietly governed. And grant unto thy
servant *Elizabeth* our Queen, and to all that are put in authority
under her, that they may truly and impartially administer justice,
to the punishment of wickedness and vice, and to the maintenance
of thy true religion and virtue.

Give grace, O heavenly Father, to all bishops, priests and deacons,
especially to thy servant *N* our bishop, that they may both by their
life and doctrine set forth thy true and lively word, and rightly and
duly administer thy holy sacraments.

Guide and prosper, we pray thee, those who are labouring for the
spread of thy gospel among the nations, and enlighten with thy Spirit
all places of education and learning; that the whole world may be
filled with the knowledge of thy truth.

And to all thy people give thy heavenly grace; and specially to this
congregation here present, that, with meek heart and due
reverence, they may hear and receive thy holy word, truly serving
thee in holiness and righteousness all the days of their life.

And we most humbly beseech thee of thy goodness, O Lord,
to comfort and succour all them who in this transitory life are
in trouble, sorrow, need, sickness, or any other adversity.

sample

And we commend to thy gracious keeping, O Lord, all thy servants
departed this life in thy faith and fear, beseeching thee, according
to thy promises, to grant them refreshment, light and peace.

And here we give thee most high praise and hearty thanks for all
thy saints, who have been the chosen vessels of thy grace, and lights
of the world in their several generations; and we pray that, rejoicing
in their fellowship and following their good examples, we may be
partakers with them of thy heavenly kingdom.

Grant this, O Father, for Jesus Christ's sake, our only mediator
and advocate.

All **Amen.**

4

*At the end of this form of intercession, silence may be kept and a collect
or other ending may be said (see page 142).*

In the power of the Spirit and in union with Christ,
let us pray to the Father.

Hear our prayers, O Lord our God.

All **Hear us, good Lord.**

Govern and direct your holy Church; fill it with love and truth;
and grant it that unity which is your will.

All **Hear us, good Lord.**

Give us boldness to preach the gospel in all the world,
and to make disciples of all the nations.

All **Hear us, good Lord.**

Enlighten *N* our bishop and all your ministers with knowledge
and understanding, that by their teaching and their lives they
may proclaim your word.

All **Hear us, good Lord.**

Give your people grace to hear and receive your word,
and to bring forth the fruit of the Spirit.

All **Hear us, good Lord.**

Bring into the way of truth all who have erred and are deceived.

All **Hear us, good Lord.**

Strengthen those who stand, comfort and help the faint-hearted;
raise up the fallen; and finally beat down Satan under our feet.

All **Hear us, good Lord.**

Guide the leaders of the nations into the ways of peace and justice.

All **Hear us, good Lord.**

Guard and strengthen your servant *Elizabeth* our Queen,
that she may put her trust in you, and seek your honour and glory.

All **Hear us, good Lord.**

Endue the High Court of Parliament and all the ministers of
the Crown with wisdom and understanding.

All **Hear us, good Lord.**

Bless those who administer the law, that they may uphold
justice, honesty and truth.

All **Hear us, good Lord.**

Give us the will to use the fruits of the earth to your glory,
and for the good of all creation.

All **Hear us, good Lord.**

Bless and keep all your people.

All **Hear us, good Lord.**

Help and comfort the lonely, the bereaved and the oppressed.

All **Lord, have mercy.**

Keep in safety those who travel, and all who are in danger.

All **Lord, have mercy.**

Heal the sick in body and mind, and provide for the homeless,
the hungry, and the destitute.

All **Lord, have mercy.**

Show your pity on prisoners and refugees, and all who are in trouble.

All **Lord, have mercy.**

Forgive our enemies, persecutors and slanderers, and turn
their hearts.

All **Lord, have mercy.**

Hear us as we remember those who have died in the peace
of Christ, both those who have confessed the faith and those
whose faith is known to you alone, and grant us with them
a share in your eternal kingdom.

All **Lord, have mercy.**

Silence may be kept and a collect or other ending may be said.

sample

5

*At the end of this form of intercession, silence may be kept and a collect
or other ending may be said (see page 142).*

In the power of the Spirit and in union with Christ,
let us pray to the Father.

For the peace of the whole world,
for the welfare of the Holy Church of God,
and for the unity of all,
let us pray to the Lord.

All   **Lord, have mercy.**

For *N* our bishop,
for the leaders of our sister Churches,
and for all clergy and people,
let us pray to the Lord.

All   **Lord, have mercy.**

For *Elizabeth* our Queen,
for the leaders of the nations,
and for all in authority,
let us pray to the Lord.

All   **Lord, have mercy.**

For this community,
for every city, town and village,
and for all the people who live within them,
let us pray to the Lord.

All   **Lord, have mercy.**

For good weather,
and for abundant harvests for all to share,
let us pray to the Lord.

All   **Lord, have mercy.**

For those who travel by land, air, or water,
for the sick and the suffering,
for ... ,
for prisoners and captives,
and for their safety, health and salvation,
let us pray to the Lord.

All   **Lord, have mercy.**

For our deliverance from all affliction, strife and need,
and for the absolution of our sins and offences,
let us pray to the Lord.

All   **Lord, have mercy.**

Remembering *(... and)*
all who have gone before us in faith,
and in communion with *(... and)* all the saints,
we commit ourselves, one another,
and our whole life to Christ our God;

All   **to you, O Lord.**

Silence may be kept and a collect or other ending may be said.

sample

¶ *Collects and Other Endings for Intercession*

For use by the president or those leading intercessions.

1

Heavenly Father,
you have promised through your Son Jesus Christ,
that when we meet in his name,
and pray according to his mind,
he will be among us and hear our prayer:
in your love and mercy fulfil our desires,
and give us your greatest gift,
which is to know you, the only true God,
and your Son Jesus Christ our Lord.

All **Amen.**

2

Be with us, Lord, in all our prayers,
and direct our way toward the attainment of salvation,
that among the changes and chances of this mortal life,
we may always be defended by your gracious help;
through Jesus Christ our Lord.

All **Amen.**

3

Almighty God, the fountain of all wisdom,
you know our needs before we ask,
and our ignorance in asking:
have compassion on our weakness,
and give us those things
which for our unworthiness we dare not,
and for our blindness we cannot ask,
for the sake of your Son Jesus Christ our Lord.

All **Amen.**

4

Almighty God,
you have promised to hear the prayers
of those who ask in your Son's name;
we pray that what we have asked faithfully
we may obtain effectually;
through Jesus Christ our Lord.

All **Amen.**

5

Almighty God,
by your Holy Spirit you have made us one
with your saints in heaven and on earth:
grant that in our earthly pilgrimage
we may ever be supported by this fellowship of love and prayer,
and know ourselves surrounded by their witness
    to your power and mercy;
through Jesus Christ our Lord.

All   **Amen.**

6

Bring us all to your heavenly city,
to the joyful gathering of thousands of angels,
to the assembly of your first-born,
to the spirits of the saints made perfect,
to Jesus the mediator of the new covenant
and to the sprinkled blood that promises peace.
Merciful Father …

All   **accept these prayers**
for the sake of your Son,
our Saviour Jesus Christ.
Amen.

7

Hasten, Lord, the day when people will come
from east and west,
from north and south,
and sit at table in your kingdom
and we shall see your Son in his glory.
Merciful Father …

8

Almighty God,
who hast given us grace at this time with one accord
to make our common supplications unto thee;
and dost promise
that when two or three are gathered together in thy name
thou wilt grant their requests:
fulfil now, O Lord, the desires and petitions of thy servants,
as may be most expedient for them;
granting us in this world knowledge of thy truth,
and in the world to come life everlasting.

All   **Amen.**

sample

¶ Introductions to the Peace

1

Christ is our peace.
He has reconciled us to God
in one body by the cross.
We meet in his name and share his peace.

2

We are the body of Christ.
In the one Spirit we were all baptized into one body.
Let us then pursue all that makes for peace
and builds up our common life.

3

May the God of peace make you perfect and holy,
that you may be kept safe and blameless
in spirit, soul and body,
for the coming of our Lord Jesus Christ.

4

Blessed are the peacemakers:
they shall be called children of God.
We meet in the name of Christ and share his peace.

5

God is love
and those who live in love live in God
and God lives in them.

6

'Where two or three are gathered together in my name,'
says the Lord, 'there am I in the midst of them.'

7

We are all one in Christ Jesus.
We belong to him through faith,
heirs of the promise of the Spirit of peace.

The provision made for seasons and principal holy days
(see pages 154–83) may be used at other times when appropriate.

¶ *Prayers at the Preparation of the Table*

1

Yours, Lord, is the greatness, the power,
the glory, the splendour, and the majesty;
for everything in heaven and on earth is yours.

All **All things come from you,
and of your own do we give you.**

2

Generous God,
creator, redeemer, sustainer,
at your table we present this money,
symbol of the work you have given us to do;
use it, use us,
in the service of your world
to the glory of your name.

All **Amen.**

3

God of life, Saviour of the poor,
receive with this money
gratitude for your goodness,
penitence for our pride
and dedication to your service
in Jesus Christ our Lord.

All **Amen.**

4

Blessed are you, Lord God of all creation:
through your goodness we have this bread to set before you,
which earth has given and human hands have made.
It will become for us the bread of life.

All **Blessed be God for ever.**

Blessed are you, Lord God of all creation:
through your goodness we have this wine to set before you,
fruit of the vine and work of human hands.
It will become for us the cup of salvation.

All **Blessed be God for ever.**

sample

5

Be present, be present,
Lord Jesus Christ,
our risen high priest;
make yourself known in the breaking of bread.

All   **Amen.**

6

As the grain once scattered in the fields
and the grapes once dispersed on the hillside
are now reunited on this table in bread and wine,
so, Lord, may your whole Church soon be gathered together
from the corners of the earth
into your kingdom.

All   **Amen.**

7

Wise and gracious God,
you spread a table before us;
nourish your people with the word of life
and the bread of heaven.

All   **Amen.**

8

*In this prayer, the texts for single voice need not be spoken by
the president. It will sometimes be appropriate to ask children to
speak them.*

With this bread that we bring

All   **we shall remember Jesus.**

With this wine that we bring

All   **we shall remember Jesus.**

Bread for his body,
wine for his blood,
gifts from God to his table we bring.

All   **We shall remember Jesus.**

9

Blessed be God,
by whose grace creation is renewed,
by whose love heaven is opened,
by whose mercy we offer our sacrifice of praise.

All **Blessed be God for ever.**

10

Blessed be God,
who feeds the hungry,
who raises the poor,
who fills our praise.

All **Blessed be God for ever.**

11

Look upon us in mercy not in judgement;
draw us from hatred to love;
make the frailty of our praise
a dwelling place for your glory.

All **Amen.**

12

Pour upon the poverty of our love,
and the weakness of our praise,
the transforming fire of your presence.

All **Amen.**

¶ *Extended Preface for the Sundays before Lent and after Trinity*

It is truly right and just, our duty and our salvation,
always and everywhere to give you thanks,
holy Father, almighty and eternal God.
From sunrise to sunset this day is holy,
for Christ has risen from the tomb
and scattered the darkness of death
with light that will not fade.
This day the risen Lord walks with your gathered people,
unfolds for us your word,
and makes himself known in the breaking of the bread.
And though the night will overtake this day
you summon us to live in endless light,
the never-ceasing sabbath of the Lord.
And so, with choirs of angels
and with all the heavenly host,
we proclaim your glory
and join their unending song of praise:

¶ *Words at the Giving of Communion*

1

The body of our Lord Jesus Christ,
which was given for you,
preserve your body and soul unto everlasting life.
Take and eat this in remembrance that Christ died for you,
and feed on him in your heart by faith with thanksgiving.

The blood of our Lord Jesus Christ,
which was shed for you,
preserve your body and soul unto everlasting life.
Drink this in remembrance that Christ's blood was shed for you,
and be thankful.

2

The body of Christ.
The blood of Christ.

3

The body of Christ keep you in eternal life.
The blood of Christ keep you in eternal life.

4

The body of Christ, broken for you.
The blood of Christ, shed for you.

5

The bread of heaven in Christ Jesus.
The cup of life in Christ Jesus.

sample

¶ Supplementary Consecration

If either or both of the consecrated elements are likely to prove insufficient, the president returns to the holy table and adds more, saying these words

Father, having given thanks over the bread and the cup
according to the institution of your Son Jesus Christ,
who said,
'Take, eat; this is my body'
(and/or 'Drink this; this is my blood'),
we pray that by the power of your Holy Spirit
this *bread/wine* also
may be to us his *body/blood,*
to be received in remembrance of him.

or (traditional language)

Father, having given thanks over the bread and the cup
according to the institution of thy Son Jesus Christ,
who said,
'Take, eat; this is my body'
(and/or 'Drink ye all of this; this is my blood'),
we pray that by the power of thy Holy Spirit
this *bread/wine* also
may be unto us his *body/blood,*
to be received in remembrance of him.

¶ *Prayers after Communion*

1

All **We thank you, Lord,**
that you have fed us in this sacrament,
united us with Christ,
and given us a foretaste of the heavenly banquet
prepared for all peoples.
Amen.

2

All **Faithful God,**
in baptism you have adopted us as your children,
made us members of the body of Christ
and chosen us as inheritors of your kingdom:
we thank you that in this Eucharist
you renew your promises within us,
empower us by your Spirit to witness and to serve,
and send us out as disciples of your Son,
Jesus Christ our Lord.
Amen.

3

All **You have opened to us the Scriptures, O Christ,**
and you have made yourself known
    in the breaking of the bread.
Abide with us, we pray,
that, blessed by your royal presence,
we may walk with you
all the days of our life,
and at its end behold you
in the glory of the eternal Trinity,
one God for ever and ever.
Amen.

4

Almighty and ever-living God,
we thank you that you graciously feed us,
who have duly received these holy mysteries,
with the spiritual food of the body and blood
    of our Saviour Jesus Christ.
By this you assure us of your favour and goodness towards us:
we are incorporated into the mystical body of your Son,
    the blessed company of all faithful people;
we are heirs, through hope, of your everlasting kingdom,
by the merits of Christ's precious death and passion.
Assist us with your grace, heavenly Father,
that we may continue in that holy fellowship,
and walk in goodness the way you have prepared for us;
through Jesus Christ our Lord,
to whom, with you and the Holy Spirit,
be all honour and glory, now and for ever.

All   **Amen.**

¶ Blessings

1

God the Father,
by whose glory Christ was raised from the dead,
strengthen you to walk with him in his risen life;
and the blessing …

2

Christ the good shepherd,
who laid down his life for the sheep,
draw you and all who hear his voice,
to be one flock within one fold;
and the blessing …

3

The God of all grace,
who called you to his eternal glory in Christ Jesus,
establish, strengthen and settle you in the faith;
and the blessing …

4

Christ, who has nourished us with himself the living bread,
make you one in praise and love,
and raise you up at the last day;
and the blessing …

5

May the Father from whom every family
in earth and heaven receives its name
strengthen you with his Spirit in your inner being,
so that Christ may dwell in your hearts by faith;
and the blessing …

6

The God of hope fill you with all joy and peace in believing;
and the blessing …

7

May God, who in Christ gives us a spring of water welling up to
eternal life,
perfect in you the image of his glory; and the blessing …

The provision made for seasons and principal holy days
(see pages 154–83) may be used at other times when appropriate.

sample

Seasonal Provisions

From the First Sunday of Advent until Christmas Eve

Invitation to Confession
When the Lord comes,
he will bring to light things now hidden in darkness,
and will disclose the purposes of the heart.
Therefore in the light of Christ let us confess our sins.

1 Corinthians 4.5

Gospel Acclamation
Alleluia, alleluia.
Prepare the way of the Lord, make his paths straight,
and all flesh shall see the salvation of God.   *cf Isaiah 40.3-5*

All **Alleluia.**

Introduction to the Peace
In the tender mercy of our God,
the dayspring from on high shall break upon us,
to give light to those who dwell in darkness
    and in the shadow of death
and to guide our feet into the way of peace.

Luke 1.78-9

Eucharistic Prefaces

Short preface (contemporary language)
And now we give you thanks
because you sent him to redeem us from sin and death
    and to make us inheritors of everlasting life;
that when he shall come again in power and great triumph
    to judge the world,
we may with joy behold his appearing,
and in confidence may stand before him.

Short preface (traditional language)
And now we give thee thanks
because thou didst send him to redeem us from sin and death
    and to make us inheritors of everlasting life;

that when he shall come again in power and great triumph
    to judge the world,
we may with joy behold his appearing,
    and in confidence may stand before him.

Extended preface for use with Eucharistic Prayers A, B and E
(from the First Sunday of Advent until 16 December)
It is indeed right and good to give you thanks and praise,
almighty God and everlasting Father,
through Jesus Christ your Son.
For when he humbled himself to come among us in human flesh,
he fulfilled the plan you formed before the foundation of the world
to open for us the way of salvation.
Confident that your promise will be fulfilled,
we now watch for the day
when Christ our Lord will come again in glory.
And so we join our voices with angels and archangels
and with all the company of heaven
to proclaim your glory,
for ever praising you and *saying*:

(from 17 December until Christmas Eve)
It is indeed right and good to give you thanks and praise,
almighty God and everlasting Father,
through Jesus Christ your Son.
He is the one foretold by all the prophets,
whom the Virgin Mother bore with love beyond all telling.
John the Baptist was his herald
and made him known when at last he came.
In his love Christ fills us with joy
as we prepare to celebrate his birth,
so that when he comes again he may find us watching in prayer,
our hearts filled with wonder and praise.
And so, with angels and archangels,
and with all the company of heaven,
we proclaim your glory,
and join in their unending hymn of praise:

Blessing
Christ the Sun of Righteousness shine upon you,
scatter the darkness from before your path,
and make you ready to meet him when he comes in glory;
and the blessing …

sample

From Christmas Day
until the Eve of the Epiphany

Invitation to Confession
Hear the words of the angel to Joseph:
'You shall call his name Jesus,
for he will save his people from their sins.'
Therefore let us seek the forgiveness of God
through Jesus the Saviour of the world.　　　　　*cf Matthew 1.21*

Gospel Acclamation
Alleluia, alleluia.
The Word became flesh and dwelt among us,
and we have seen his glory.　　　　　*John 1.14*

All　**Alleluia.**

Introduction to the Peace
Unto us a child is born, unto us a son is given,
and his name shall be called the Prince of Peace.　　　　　*Isaiah 9.6*

Eucharistic Prefaces

Short preface (contemporary language)
And now we give you thanks
because, by the power of the Holy Spirit,
he took our nature upon him
and was born of the Virgin Mary his mother,
that being himself without sin,
he might make us clean from all sin.

Short preface (traditional language)
And now we give thee thanks
because, by the power of the Holy Spirit,
he took our nature upon him
and was born of the Virgin Mary his mother,
that being himself without sin,
he might make us clean from all sin.

Extended preface for use with Eucharistic Prayers A, B and E
All glory and honour be yours always and everywhere,
mighty creator, ever-living God.
We give you thanks and praise for your Son,
our Saviour Jesus Christ,
who for love of our fallen race humbled himself,
was born of the Virgin Mary by the power of your Spirit,
and lived as one of us.
In this mystery of the Word made flesh
you have caused his light to shine in our hearts,
to give knowledge of your glory in the face of Jesus Christ.
In him we see our God made visible
and so are caught up in the love of the God we cannot see.
Therefore with all the angels of heaven
we lift our voices to proclaim the glory of your name
and sing our joyful hymn of praise:

Blessing
Christ, who by his incarnation gathered into one
    things earthly and heavenly,
fill you with peace and goodwill
and make you partakers of the divine nature;
and the blessing …

sample

From the Epiphany
until the Eve of the Presentation

Invitation to Confession
The grace of God has dawned upon the world
    through our Saviour Jesus Christ,
      who sacrificed himself for us to purify a people as his own.
Let us confess our sins.   *Titus 2.11-14*

Gospel Acclamation
Alleluia, alleluia.
Christ was revealed in flesh, proclaimed among the nations
and believed in throughout the world.   *cf 1 Timothy 3.16*

All   **Alleluia.**

Introduction to the Peace
Our Saviour Christ is the Prince of Peace.
Of the increase of his government and of peace
there shall be no end.   *cf Isaiah 9.6-7*

Eucharistic Prefaces

Short preface (contemporary language)
And now we give you thanks
because, in the incarnation of the Word,
a new light has dawned upon the world,
that all the nations may be brought out of darkness
to see the radiance of your glory.

Short preface (traditional language)
And now we give thee thanks
because, in the incarnation of the Word,
a new light has dawned upon the world,
that all the nations may be brought out of darkness
to see the radiance of thy glory.

Extended preface for use with Eucharistic Prayers A, B and E
All honour and praise be yours always and everywhere,
mighty creator, ever-living God,
through Jesus Christ your only Son our Lord:
for at this time we celebrate your glory
made present in our midst.
In the coming of the Magi
the King of all the world was revealed to the nations.
In the waters of baptism
Jesus was revealed as the Christ,
the Saviour sent to redeem us.
In the water made wine
the new creation was revealed at the wedding feast.
Poverty was turned to riches, sorrow into joy.
Therefore with all the angels of heaven
we lift our voices to proclaim the glory of your name
and sing our joyful hymn of praise:

Blessing
Christ the Son of God perfect in you the image of his glory
and gladden your hearts with the good news of his kingdom;
and the blessing ...

The Presentation of Christ in the Temple

Invitation to Confession
Hear the words of our Saviour Jesus Christ:
'I am the light of the world.
Whoever follows me shall never walk in darkness
but shall have the light of life.'
Let us therefore bring our sins into his light
and confess them in penitence and faith.   *cf John 8.12*

Gospel Acclamation
Alleluia, alleluia.
This child is the light to enlighten the nations,
and the glory of your people Israel.   *cf Luke 2.32*

All **Alleluia.**

Introduction to the Peace
In the tender mercy of our God
the dayspring from on high has broken upon us,
to give light to those who dwell in darkness
    and in the shadow of death
and to guide our feet into the way of peace.   *cf Luke 1.78-9*

Eucharistic Prefaces

Short preface (contemporary language)
And now we give you thanks
because, by appearing in the temple,
he comes near to us in judgement;
the Word made flesh searches the hearts of all your people
and brings to light the brightness of your splendour.

Short preface (traditional language)
And now we give thee thanks
because, by appearing in the temple,
he comes near to us in judgement;
the Word made flesh searches the hearts of all thy people
and brings to light the brightness of thy splendour.

Extended preface for use with Eucharistic Prayers A, B and E
It is indeed right and good,
always and everywhere to give you thanks and praise
through Jesus Christ, who is one with you from all eternity.
For on this day he appeared in the temple
in substance of our flesh
to come near to us in judgement.
He searches the hearts of all your people
and brings to light the image of your splendour.
Your servant Simeon acclaimed him as the light to lighten the nations
while Anna spoke of him to all who looked for your redemption.
Destined for the falling and rising of many,
he was lifted high upon the cross
and a sword of sorrow pierced his mother's heart
when by his sacrifice he made our peace with you.
And now we rejoice and glorify your name
that we, too, have seen your salvation
and join with angels and archangels
in their unending hymn of praise:

Blessing
Christ the Son of God, born of Mary,
fill you with his grace to trust his promises and obey his will;
and the blessing ...

sample

From Ash Wednesday
until the Saturday after
the Fourth Sunday of Lent

Invitation to Confession
The sacrifice of God is a broken spirit;
a broken and contrite heart God will not despise.
Let us come to the Lord, who is full of compassion,
and acknowledge our transgressions in penitence and faith.

cf Psalm 51.17

Gospel Acclamation
Praise to you, O Christ, King of eternal glory.
The Lord is a great God, O that today you would listen to his voice.
Harden not your hearts.   *cf Psalm 95.3,7-8*

All **Praise to you, O Christ, King of eternal glory.**

Introduction to the Peace
Since we are justified by faith,
we have peace with God through our Lord Jesus Christ,
who has given us access to his grace.   *Romans 5.1-2*

Eucharistic Prefaces

Short preface (contemporary language)
And now we give you thanks
because you give us the spirit of discipline,
that we may triumph over evil and grow in grace,
as we prepare to celebrate the paschal mystery
    with mind and heart renewed.

Short preface (traditional language)
And now we give thee thanks
because thou dost give us the spirit of discipline,
that we may triumph over evil and grow in grace,
as we prepare to celebrate the paschal mystery
    with mind and heart renewed.

Extended preface for use with Eucharistic Prayers A, B and E
It is indeed right and good
to give you thanks and praise,
almighty God and everlasting Father,
through Jesus Christ your Son.
For in these forty days
you lead us into the desert of repentance
that through a pilgrimage of prayer and discipline
we may grow in grace
and learn to be your people once again.
Through fasting, prayer and acts of service
you bring us back to your generous heart.
Through study of your holy word
you open our eyes to your presence in the world
and free our hands to welcome others
into the radiant splendour of your love.
As we prepare to celebrate the Easter feast
with joyful hearts and minds
we bless you for your mercy
and join with saints and angels
for ever praising you and *saying*:

Blessing
Christ give you grace to grow in holiness,
to deny yourselves, take up your cross, and follow him;
and the blessing ...

sample

The Annunciation of Our Lord

Invitation to Confession
The grace of God has dawned upon the world
    through our Saviour Jesus Christ,
      who sacrificed himself for us to purify a people as his own.
Let us confess our sins.   *Titus 2.11-14*

Gospel Acclamation
Praise to you, O Christ, King of eternal glory.
The Word became flesh and lived among us,
and we have seen his glory.   *John 1.14*

All   **Praise to you, O Christ, King of eternal glory.**

*(Note: If the Annunciation falls in Eastertide, use the text provided
for Christmas.)*

Introduction to the Peace
In the tender mercy of our God,
the dayspring from on high shall break upon us,
to give light to those who dwell in darkness
    and in the shadow of death
and to guide our feet into the way of peace.   *Luke 1.78-9*
(In Eastertide, add Alleluia.)

Eucharistic Prefaces

Short preface (contemporary language)
And now we give you thanks
because, by the power of the Holy Spirit,
he took our nature upon him
and was born of the Virgin Mary his mother,
that being himself without sin,
he might make us clean from all sin.

Short preface (traditional language)
And now we give thee thanks
because, by the power of the Holy Spirit,
he took our nature upon him
and was born of the Virgin Mary his mother,
that being himself without sin,
he might make us clean from all sin.

Extended preface for use with Eucharistic Prayers A, B and E
It is indeed right and good,
our duty and our salvation,
always and everywhere to give you thanks,
holy Father, almighty and eternal God,
through Jesus Christ your Son our Lord.
We give you thanks and praise
that the Virgin Mary heard with faith the message of the angel,
and by the power of your Holy Spirit
conceived and bore the Word made flesh.
From the warmth of her womb
to the stillness of the grave
he shared our life in human form.
In him new light has dawned upon the world
and you have become one with us
that we might become one with you
in your glorious kingdom.
Therefore earth unites with heaven
to sing a new song of praise;
we too join with angels and archangels
as they proclaim your glory without end:

Blessing
Christ the Son of God, born of Mary,
fill you with his grace to trust his promises and obey his will;
and the blessing ...

From the Fifth Sunday of Lent
until the Wednesday of Holy Week

Invitation to Confession
God shows his love for us
    in that, while we were still sinners, Christ died for us.
Let us then show our love for him
by confessing our sins in penitence and faith.   *Romans 5.8*

Gospel Acclamation
Praise to you, O Christ, King of eternal glory.
Christ humbled himself and became obedient unto death,
even death on a cross.
Therefore God has highly exalted him
and given him the name that is above every name.   *Philippians 2.8-9*

All   **Praise to you, O Christ, King of eternal glory.**

Introduction to the Peace
Once we were far off,
but now in union with Christ Jesus we have been brought near
    through the shedding of Christ's blood,
for he is our peace.   *Ephesians 2.13*

Eucharistic Prefaces

Short preface (contemporary language)
And now we give you thanks
because, for our salvation,
he was obedient even to death on the cross.
The tree of shame was made the tree of glory;
and where life was lost, there life has been restored.

Short preface (traditional language)
And now we give thee thanks
because, for our salvation,
he was obedient even to death on the cross.
The tree of shame was made the tree of glory;
and where life was lost, there life has been restored.

Extended preface for use with Eucharistic Prayers A, B and E
It is indeed right and just,
our duty and our salvation,
always and everywhere to give you thanks,
holy Father, almighty and eternal God,
through Jesus Christ our Lord.
For as the time of his passion and resurrection draws near
the whole world is called to acknowledge his hidden majesty.
The power of the life-giving cross
reveals the judgement that has come upon the world
and the triumph of Christ crucified.
He is the victim who dies no more,
the Lamb once slain, who lives for ever,
our advocate in heaven to plead our cause,
exalting us there to join with angels and archangels,
for ever praising you and *saying*:

Blessing
Christ crucified draw you to himself,
to find in him a sure ground for faith,
a firm support for hope,
and the assurance of sins forgiven;
and the blessing …

sample

Maundy Thursday

Invitation to Confession
Our Lord Jesus Christ says:
'If you love me, keep my commandments.'
'Unless I wash you, you have no part in me.'
Let us confess to almighty God our sins against his love,
and ask him to cleanse us.   *cf John 14.15; 13.8*

Gospel Acclamation
Praise to you, O Christ, King of eternal glory.
I give you a new commandment, says the Lord:
Love one another as I have loved you.   *cf John 13.34*

All **Praise to you, O Christ, King of eternal glory.**

Introduction to the Peace
Jesus says: 'Peace I leave with you; my peace I give to you.
Do not let your hearts be troubled, neither let them be afraid.'
                                            cf John 14.27

Eucharistic Prefaces

Short preface (contemporary language)
And now we give you thanks
because, having loved his own who were in the world,
he loved them to the end;
and on the night before he suffered,
sitting at table with his disciples,
he instituted these holy mysteries,
that we, redeemed by his death
    and restored to life by his resurrection,
might be partakers of his divine nature.

Short preface (traditional language)
And now we give thee thanks
because, having loved his own who were in the world,
he loved them to the end;
and on the night before he suffered,
sitting at table with his disciples,
he instituted these holy mysteries,
that we, redeemed by his death
    and restored to life by his resurrection,
might be partakers of his divine nature.

Extended preface for use with Eucharistic Prayers A, B and E
It is indeed right to give you thanks,
Father most holy, through Jesus Christ our Lord.
For on this night he girded himself with a towel
and, taking the form of a servant,
washed the feet of his disciples.
He gave us a new commandment
that we should love one another as he has loved us.
Knowing that his hour had come,
in his great love he gave this supper to his disciples
to be a memorial of his passion,
that we might proclaim his death until he comes again,
and feast with him in his kingdom.
Therefore earth unites with heaven
to sing a new song of praise;
we too join with angels and archangels
as they proclaim your glory without end:

There is no blessing at the end of the Maundy Thursday liturgy.

sample

From Easter Day
until the Eve of the Ascension

Invitation to Confession
Christ our passover lamb has been sacrificed for us.
Let us therefore rejoice by putting away all malice and evil
and confessing our sins with a sincere and true heart.

1 Corinthians 5.7-8

Gospel Acclamation
Alleluia, alleluia.
I am the first and the last, says the Lord, and the living one;
I was dead, and behold I am alive for evermore.

All **Alleluia.** *cf Revelation 1.17-18*

Introduction to the Peace
The risen Christ came and stood among his disciples
 and said, 'Peace be with you.'
Then were they glad when they saw the Lord. Alleluia.

John 20.19-20

Eucharistic Prefaces

Short preface (contemporary language)
But chiefly are we bound to praise you
because you raised him gloriously from the dead.
For he is the true paschal lamb who was offered for us,
and has taken away the sin of the world.
By his death he has destroyed death,
and by his rising to life again he has restored to us everlasting life.

Short preface (traditional language)
But chiefly are we bound to praise thee
because thou didst raise him gloriously from the dead.
For he is the true paschal lamb who was offered for us,
and has taken away the sin of the world.
By his death he has destroyed death,
and by his rising to life again he has restored to us everlasting life.

Extended preface for use with Eucharistic Prayers A, B and E
It is indeed right, our duty and our joy,
always and everywhere to give you thanks,
almighty and eternal Father,
and in these days of Easter
to celebrate with joyful hearts
the memory of your wonderful works.
For by the mystery of his passion
Jesus Christ, your risen Son,
has conquered the powers of death and hell
and restored in men and women the image of your glory.
He has placed them once more in paradise
and opened to them the gate of life eternal.
And so, in the joy of this Passover,
earth and heaven resound with gladness,
while angels and archangels and the powers of all creation
sing for ever the hymn of your glory:

Blessing
The God of peace,
who brought again from the dead our Lord Jesus,
that great shepherd of the sheep,
through the blood of the eternal covenant,
make you perfect in every good work to do his will,
working in you that which is well-pleasing in his sight;
and the blessing ...

Ascension Day

Invitation to Confession

Seeing we have a great high priest who has passed into the heavens,
   Jesus the Son of God,
let us draw near with a true heart, in full assurance of faith,
and make our confession to our heavenly Father.

Hebrews 4.14; 10.22

Gospel Acclamation
Alleluia, alleluia.
Go and make disciples of all nations, says the Lord.
Remember, I am with you always, to the end of the age.

All **Alleluia.**   *cf Matthew 28.19-20*

Introduction to the Peace
Jesus says: 'Peace I leave with you; my peace I give to you.
If you love me, rejoice because I am going to the Father.' Alleluia.

John 14.27-8

Eucharistic Prefaces

Short preface (contemporary language)
And now we give you thanks
because, after his most glorious resurrection,
he appeared to his disciples,
and in their sight ascended into heaven to prepare a place for us;
that where he is, thither we might also ascend,
and reign with him in glory.

Short preface (traditional language)
And now we give thee thanks
because, after his most glorious resurrection,
he appeared to his disciples,
and in their sight ascended into heaven to prepare a place for us;
that where he is, thither we might also ascend,
and reign with him in glory.

Extended preface for use with Eucharistic Prayers A, B and E
It is indeed right and good,
our duty and our joy,
always and everywhere to give you thanks,
holy Father, almighty and eternal God,
through Jesus Christ the King of glory.
Born of a woman,
he came to the rescue of our human race.
Dying for us,
he trampled death and conquered sin.
By the glory of his resurrection
he opened the way to life eternal
and by his ascension,
gave us the sure hope
that where he is we may also be.
Therefore the universe resounds with Easter joy
and with choirs of angels we sing for ever to your praise:

Blessing
Christ our ascended King pour upon you the abundance of his gifts
    and bring you to reign with him in glory;
and the blessing ...

From the day after Ascension Day
until the Day of Pentecost

Invitation to Confession
What God has prepared for those who love him,
he has revealed to us through the Spirit;
for the Spirit searches everything.
Therefore, let us in penitence open our hearts to the Lord,
who has prepared good things for those who love him.

1 Corinthians 2.9-10

Gospel Acclamation
Alleluia, alleluia.
Come, Holy Spirit, fill the hearts of your faithful people
and kindle in them the fire of your love.

All **Alleluia.**

Introduction to the Peace
God has made us one in Christ.
He has set his seal upon us and, as a pledge of what is to come,
has given the Spirit to dwell in our hearts. Alleluia.

cf 2 Corinthians 1.22

Eucharistic Prefaces

Short preface (contemporary language)
And now we give you thanks
that, after he had ascended far above all heavens,
and was seated at the right hand of your majesty,
he sent forth upon the universal Church your holy and
   life-giving Spirit;
that through his glorious power the joy of the everlasting gospel
   might go forth into all the world.

Short preface (traditional language)
And now we give thee thanks
that, after he had ascended far above all heavens,
and was seated at the right hand of thy majesty,
he sent forth upon the universal Church thy holy and life-giving Spirit;
that through his glorious power the joy of the everlasting gospel
   might go forth into all the world.

Extended preface for use with Eucharistic Prayers A, B and E on days
between Ascension Day and Pentecost

It is indeed right, our duty and our joy,
always and everywhere to give you thanks,
holy Father, almighty and eternal God,
through Jesus Christ our Lord.
For he is our great high priest
who has entered once for all
into the heavenly sanctuary,
evermore to pour upon your Church
the grace and comfort of your Holy Spirit.
He is the one who has gone before us,
who calls us to be united in prayer
as were his disciples in the upper room
while they awaited his promised gift,
the life-giving Spirit of Pentecost.
Therefore all creation yearns with eager longing
as angels and archangels sing the endless hymn of praise:

(on the Day of Pentecost only)
It is indeed right, it is our duty and our joy,
always and everywhere to give you thanks,
holy Father, almighty and everlasting God,
through Jesus Christ, your only Son our Lord.
This day we give you thanks
because in fulfilment of your promise
you pour out your Spirit upon us,
filling us with your gifts, leading us into all truth,
and uniting peoples of many tongues in the confession of one faith.
Your Spirit gives us grace to call you Father,
to proclaim your gospel to all nations
and to serve you as a royal priesthood.
Therefore we join our voices with angels and archangels,
and with all those in whom the Spirit dwells,
to proclaim the glory of your name,
for ever praising you and *saying*:

Blessing
The Spirit of truth lead you into all truth,
give you grace to confess that Jesus Christ is Lord,
and strengthen you to proclaim the word and works of God;
and the blessing …

sample

Trinity Sunday

Invitation to Confession
God the Father forgives us in Christ and heals us by the Holy Spirit.
Let us therefore put away all anger and bitterness,
    all slander and malice,
and confess our sins to God our redeemer.   *cf Ephesians 4.30,32*

Gospel Acclamation
Alleluia, alleluia.
Glory to the Father, and to the Son, and to the Holy Spirit,
one God, who was, and who is, and who is to come,
the Almighty.   *cf Revelation 1.8*

All   **Alleluia.**

Introduction to the Peace
Peace to you from God our heavenly Father.
Peace from his Son Jesus Christ who is our peace.
Peace from the Holy Spirit, the life-giver.
The peace of the triune God be always with you.

Eucharistic Prefaces

Short preface (contemporary language)
And now we give you thanks
because you have revealed the glory of your eternal fellowship
    of love with your Son and with the Holy Spirit,
three persons equal in majesty, undivided in splendour,
yet one God,
ever to be worshipped and adored.

Short preface (traditional language)
And now we give thee thanks
because thou hast revealed the glory of thine eternal fellowship
    of love with thy Son and with the Holy Spirit,
three persons equal in majesty, undivided in splendour,
yet one God,
ever to be worshipped and adored.

Extended preface for use with Eucharistic Prayers A, B and E
It is indeed right, our duty and our joy,
always and everywhere to give you thanks,
holy Father, almighty and eternal God.
For with your only-begotten Son and the Holy Spirit
you are one God, one Lord.
All that you reveal of your glory,
the same we believe of the Son
and of the Holy Spirit, without any difference or inequality.
We, your holy Church, acclaim you,
Father of majesty unbounded,
your true and only Son, worthy of all worship,
and the Holy Spirit, advocate and guide.
Three Persons we adore,
one in being and equal in majesty.
And so with angels and archangels,
with cherubim and seraphim,
we sing for ever of your glory:

Blessing
God the Holy Trinity make you strong in faith and love,
defend you on every side, and guide you in truth and peace;
and the blessing …

All Saints' Day

Invitation to Confession
Since we are surrounded by a great cloud of witnesses,
let us also lay aside every weight and the sin that clings so closely,
looking to Jesus in penitence and faith.   *Hebrews 12.1*

Gospel Acclamation
Alleluia, alleluia.
You are a chosen race, a royal priesthood,
a holy nation, God's own people,
called out of darkness into his marvellous light.   *1 Peter 2.9*

All   **Alleluia.**

Introduction to the Peace
We are fellow-citizens with the saints and of the household of God,
through Christ our Lord, who came and preached peace
    to those who were far off and those who were near.
                                Ephesians 2.19,17

Eucharistic Prefaces

Short preface (contemporary language)
And now we give you thanks
for the glorious pledge of the hope of our calling
    which you have given us in your saints;
that, following their example and strengthened by their fellowship,
we may run with perseverance the race that is set before us,
and with them receive the unfading crown of glory.

Short preface (traditional language)
And now we give thee thanks
for the glorious pledge of the hope of our calling
    which thou hast given us in thy saints;
that, following their example and strengthened by their fellowship,
we may run with perseverance the race that is set before us,
and with them receive the unfading crown of glory.

Extended preface for use with Eucharistic Prayers A, B and E
It is indeed right, our duty and our joy,
always and everywhere to give you thanks,
holy Father, almighty and eternal God,
through Jesus Christ our Lord.
And now we give you thanks, most gracious God,
surrounded by a great cloud of witnesses
and glorified in the assembly of your saints.
The glorious company of apostles praise you.
The noble fellowship of prophets praise you.
The white-robed army of martyrs praise you.
We, your holy Church, acclaim you.
In communion with angels and archangels,
and with all who served you on earth
and worship you now in heaven,
we raise our voice to proclaim your glory,
for ever praising you and *saying*:

Blessing
God, who has prepared for us a city with eternal foundations,
give you grace to share the inheritance of the saints in glory;
and the blessing …

From the day after All Saints' Day until the day before the First Sunday of Advent

Invitation to Confession
Jesus says, 'Repent, for the kingdom of heaven is close at hand.'
So let us turn away from sin and turn to Christ,
confessing our sins in penitence and faith.   *Mark 1.14*

Gospel Acclamation
Alleluia, alleluia.
Blessed is the king who comes in the name of the Lord.
Peace in heaven and glory in the highest heaven.   *Luke 19.38*

All **Alleluia.**

Introduction to the Peace
To crown all things there must be love,
to bind all together and complete the whole.
Let the peace of Christ rule in our hearts.   *Colossians 3.14-15*

Eucharistic Prefaces

Short preface (contemporary language)
And now we give you thanks
that he is the King of glory,
who overcomes the sting of death
and opens the kingdom of heaven to all believers.
He is seated at your right hand in glory
and we believe that he will come to be our judge.

Short preface (traditional language)
And now we give thee thanks
that he is the King of glory,
who overcomes the sting of death
and opens the kingdom of heaven to all believers.
He is seated at thy right hand in glory
and we believe that he will come to be our judge.

Extended preface for use with Eucharistic Prayers A, B and E
It is indeed right, our duty and our joy
that we should always sing of your glory,
holy Father, almighty and eternal God,
through Jesus Christ your Son our Lord.
For you are the hope of the nations,
the builder of the city that is to come.
Your love made visible in Jesus Christ
brings home the lost,
restores the sinner
and gives dignity to the despised.
In his face your light shines out,
flooding lives with goodness and truth,
gathering into one in your kingdom
a divided and broken humanity.
Therefore with all who can give voice in your creation
we glorify your name,
for ever praising you and *saying*:

(on the feast of Christ the King only)
It is indeed right, our duty and our joy,
always and everywhere to give you thanks,
holy Father, almighty and eternal God.
For with the oil of gladness
you have anointed Christ the Lord, your only Son,
to be our great high priest and king of all creation.
As priest, he offered himself once for all upon the altar of the cross
and redeemed the human race by this perfect sacrifice of peace.
As king he claims dominion over all your creatures,
that he may bring before your infinite majesty
a kingdom of truth and life,
a kingdom of holiness and grace,
a kingdom of justice, love and peace.
And so with angels and archangels
and all the heavenly host,
we proclaim your glory
and join in their unending hymn of praise:

Blessing
Christ our King make you faithful and strong to do his will,
that you may reign with him in glory;
and the blessing ...

sample

On Saints' Days

Invitation to Confession
The saints were faithful unto death
and now dwell in the heavenly kingdom for ever.
As we celebrate their joy,
let us bring to the Lord our sins and weaknesses,
and ask for his mercy.

Gospel Acclamation
Alleluia, alleluia.
I have called you friends, says the Lord,
for all that I have heard from my Father
I have made known to you.   *cf John 15.15*

All **Alleluia.**

or, in Lent
Praise to you, O Christ, King of eternal glory.
I have called you friends, says the Lord,
for all that I have heard from my Father
I have made known to you.   *cf John 15.15*

All **Praise to you, O Christ, King of eternal glory.**

Introduction to the Peace
May the God of peace sanctify you:
may he so strengthen your hearts in holiness
that you may be blameless before him
at the coming of our Lord Jesus with his saints.
                                                  1 Thessalonians 5.23; 3.13

Eucharistic Prefaces

Short preface (contemporary language)
And now we give you thanks
that your glory is revealed in (*N and*) all the saints.
In their lives you have given us an example of faithfulness to Christ.
In their holiness we find encouragement and hope.
In our communion with them we share the unity of your kingdom.

Short preface (traditional language)
And now we give thee thanks
that thy glory is revealed in (*N and*) all the saints.
In their lives thou hast given us an example of faithfulness to Christ.
In their holiness we find encouragement and hope.
In our communion with them we share the unity of thy kingdom.

Extended preface for use with Eucharistic Prayers A, B and E
It is indeed right, our duty and our joy,
always and everywhere to give you thanks,
holy Father, almighty and eternal God,
through Jesus Christ your Son our Lord.
We rejoice in the glorious splendour of your majesty
for you have given us a share with *N*
in the inheritance of the saints in light.
In the darkness of this passing age
they proclaim the glory of your kingdom.
Chosen as lights in the world,
they surround our steps as we journey on
towards the city of eternal light
where they sing the everlasting song of triumph.
In communion with angels and archangels
and all who have served you on earth
and worship you now in heaven,
we raise our voices to proclaim your glory,
for ever praising you and *saying*:

Blessing
God give you grace to follow his saints
in faith and hope and love;
and the blessing …

Notes

Notes 1 to 23 apply to Order One. They should be followed in Order Two insofar as they are applicable. Notes 24 to 29 apply to Order Two only.

The use of a lighter typeface for some texts reflects a decision of the General Synod to give more weight to one choice within a range of options.

1   **Posture**
Local custom may be followed and developed in relation to posture. The people should stand for the reading of the Gospel, for the Creed, for the Peace and for the Dismissal. Any changes in posture during the Eucharistic Prayer should not detract from the essential unity of that prayer. It is appropriate that, on occasions, the congregation should kneel for prayers of penitence.

2   **Traditional Texts**
In addition to the places where they are printed in the service, traditional versions of texts may be used.

3   **Hymns, Psalms, Canticles, the Collection and Presentation of the Offerings of the People, and the Preparation of the Gifts of Bread and Wine**
Points are indicated for these, but they may occur elsewhere.

4   **Sentences**
Sentences of Scripture appropriate to the season and the place in the service may be used as part of the president's greeting, in the invitation to confession, at the Peace, before the gifts of the people are collected and after the distribution of communion (from Easter Day to Pentecost 'Alleluia' is appropriately added to such sentences).

5   **Acclamations**
Acclamations, which may include congregational response (such as 'The Lord is here: his Spirit is with us' and 'Christ is risen: he is risen indeed') may be used at appropriate points in the service (with 'Alleluia' except in Lent). Seasonal acclamations for use before the Gospel are provided on pages 134 and 154–83.

6   **Entry**
     At the entry of the ministers, a Bible or Book of the Gospels may be
     carried into the assembly.

7   **Greetings**
     In addition to the points where greetings are provided, at other
     suitable points (e.g. before the Gospel and before the blessing or
     dismissal), the greeting 'The Lord be with you' with its response
     'and also with you' or 'and with thy spirit' may be used.

8   **Silence**
     Silence is particularly appropriate within the prayers of penitence
     and of intercession, before the collect, in response to the reading of
     the Scriptures, after the Eucharistic Prayer and after the distribution.

9   **Notices**
     Banns of marriage and other notices may be published before the
     preparation (if possible by a minister other than the president),
     before the prayers of intercession or before the dismissal.

10   **The Prayers of Penitence**
     This section may be transposed to a later point in the service as a
     response to the Liturgy of the Word. In the special seasonal rites for
     certain days it is particularly appropriate at the later point.
         On certain occasions, for a special service, this section may
     precede the opening hymn and greeting. A Form of Preparation is
     provided on page 11.
         The invitation to confession may take the form of the Summary
     of the Law, the Commandments, the Beatitudes, the Comfortable
     Words or the Exhortation.
         When the Kyrie Eleison is used as a confession, short penitential
     sentences are inserted between the petitions, suitable for seasons
     or themes. This form of confession should not be the norm on
     Sundays.
         Authorized alternative forms of confession and absolution may
     be used in place of those in the main text.

11   **Gloria in Excelsis**
     This canticle may be omitted during Advent and Lent, and on
     weekdays which are not principal holy days or festivals.
     See also note 3.

sample

12   The Readings

The readings at Holy Communion are governed by authorized lectionary provision, and are not a matter for local decision except where that provision permits.

Whenever possible, all three readings are used at Holy Communion on Sundays. When only two are read, the minister should ensure that, in any year, a balance is maintained between readings from the Old and New Testament in the choice of the first reading. The psalm provided relates to the first reading in the lectionary. Where possible it should be used after that reading.

When announcing the Gospel, if it is desired to give book, chapter and verse or page number, the reader may do this informally before saying 'Hear the Gospel of our Lord Jesus Christ according to N.'

13   The Sermon

The sermon is an integral part of the Liturgy of the Word. A sermon should normally be preached at all celebrations on Sundays and principal holy days.

The sermon may on occasion include less formal exposition of Scripture, the use of drama, interviews, discussion, and audio-visual aids.

14   The Creed

The Creed may be preceded by the president saying 'Let us declare our faith in God, Father, Son and Holy Spirit'.

15   The Prayers of Intercession

Intercession frequently arises out of thanksgiving; nevertheless these prayers are primarily prayers of intercession. They are normally broadly based, expressing a concern for the whole of God's world and the ministry of the whole Church.

Several forms of intercession are provided; other suitable forms may be used. They need not always conform to the sequence indicated.

Prayer for the nation is properly focused in prayer for the Sovereign by name, and prayer for the Church in prayer for the Bishop of the diocese by name.

The supplementary texts provide a number of collects and other endings to conclude intercession. In some circumstances it may be appropriate for the president to say both the opening invitation and these concluding words.

16 The Peace

The Peace follows naturally from the prayers of intercession and begins the Liturgy of the Sacrament. But this section may be transposed to be the opening greeting or may be used later in the service, as part of either the breaking of bread or the Dismissal. Introductions can be found in the supplementary texts.

17 The Taking

In Holy Communion the Church, following the example of the Lord, takes, gives thanks, breaks and gives. The bread and wine must be taken into the president's hands and replaced upon the table either after the table has been prepared or during the Eucharistic Prayer.

18 The Eucharistic Prefaces and Optional Acclamations

Short prefaces may be inserted in Eucharistic Prayers A, B and C in Order One, and in both prayers in Order One in Traditional Language. Texts of these are to be found on pages 154–83.

When the short prefaces given on pages 154–83 are used with Order Two and Order Two in Contemporary Language the phrase 'through Jesus Christ our Lord' must be inserted.

Extended prefaces may be used with Eucharistic Prayers A, B and E for Order One (pages 148 and 154–83). When an extended preface is used it replaces the entire text between the opening dialogue and the text of the *Sanctus*. It will be noted that in Prayer E the short text provided on page 48 must be used if no extended preface is used.

There are optional acclamations suggested for use in Prayers A and F. Those provided for Prayer F echo the style of those in the Liturgy of St Basil and might, especially when sung, be led by a deacon or minister other than the president, then repeated by the whole congregation. Other acclamations may be used.

19 The Lord's Prayer

On any occasion when the text of an alternative service authorized under the provisions of Canon B 2 provides for the Lord's Prayer to be said or sung, it may be used in the form included in *The Book of Common Prayer* or in either of the two other forms included in services in *Common Worship*. The text included in Prayers for Various Occasions (page 00) may be used on suitable occasions.

sample

20 Breaking of the Bread

Sufficient bread for the whole congregation to share may be broken by the president, if necessary assisted by other ministers, at this point in the service. Agnus Dei may accompany this action.

The words provided at the breaking of the bread must be used on Sundays and principal holy days. On other days the bread may be broken in silence or during Agnus Dei.

21 Non-communicants

At the distribution, any of those distributing the sacrament, ordained or lay, may pray for any non-communicants who come forward in these or other suitable words: 'May God be with you' or 'May God bless you'.

22 Prayers after Communion

One or two prayers may be used after Communion. If two are used, the first is normally a presidential text, the second a congregational text. If only one is used, either a presidential or congregational text is chosen. The presidential text is normally the authorized post communion of the day. The congregational text is normally one of those printed in the main text or one of those in the supplementary texts.

23 A Service without Communion

When there is no Communion, the minister leads the service as far as the prayers of intercession or the Peace, and then adds the Lord's Prayer, the General Thanksgiving, and/or other prayers, ending with the Grace.

The following notes apply to Order Two only

Frequently used additions to the text of The Book of Common Prayer *are included in Order Two but are indented from the left hand margin.*

24 Posture
It is appropriate for the people to kneel for the opening prayer and Commandments, the prayers of intercession, the confession, absolution and Comfortable Words, the Prayer of Consecration and prayers after the distribution.

25 Supplementary Material
Supplementary Texts may be used with Order Two when they are compatible with that Order. The third form of intercession in the Supplementary Texts (page 137) may be used in place of the form printed.

26 The Sermon
At the discretion of the priest, the sermon may precede the Creed.

27 Alternative Order
Where customary, the prayer of humble access may precede 'Lift up your hearts'; 'Amen' may be omitted at the end of the prayer of consecration, and the prayer of oblation follow immediately; the Lord's Prayer may follow the prayer of oblation; the versicle 'The peace of the Lord be always with you' with the response 'And with thy spirit' may follow the Lord's Prayer and precede Agnus Dei. In Order Two, but not in Order Two in Contemporary Language, the breaking of the bread may be deferred until Agnus Dei.

28 Proper Prefaces
The short proper prefaces in the Supplementary Texts (pages 154–83) may be used with Order Two. In such case the priest inserts the words 'through Jesus Christ our Lord' after 'almighty, everlasting God'. The texts of the proper prefaces from *The Book of Common Prayer* for use with Order Two are given on pages 100–1.

29 Gloria in Excelsis
If the Gloria in Excelsis is not to be used on every occasion, it is appropriately omitted on Sundays in Advent and Lent and on all weekdays that are not principal holy days or festivals.

sample

Acknowledgements

The publisher gratefully acknowledges permission to reproduce copyright material in this book. Every effort has been made to trace and contact copyright holders. If there are any inadvertent omissions we apologise to those concerned and undertake to include suitable acknowledgements in all future editions.

Published sources include the following:

The texts of the Nicene Creed (adapted), the Gloria in Excelsis, the Sanctus and Benedictus, and the Agnus Dei, as they appear in the Holy Communion Order 1 and the Apostles' Creed (adapted) in its modern form are copyright © International Consultation on English Texts (International Consultation on English Texts). The Lord's Prayer in its modern form is adapted from the International Consultation on English Texts version.

The text of *The Book of Common Prayer* is the property of the Crown in perpetuity; material from *The Book of Common Prayer* (some in adapted form) is reproduced by permission.

Thanks are also due to the following for permission to reproduce copyright material:

Canterbury Press Norwich: for the extended preface for Easter Day (p. 171); taken from *We Give You Thanks and Praise* by Alan Griffiths.

Grove Books Ltd, Ridley Hall Road, Cambridge CB3 9HU: for Collects and Other Endings for Intercession nos 6 and 7 (p. 143), from *Intercessions in the Eucharist* (Grove Booklet 77, 1982).

The International Commission on English in the Liturgy: for the extended prefaces for the Sundays before Lent and the Sundays after Trinity (p. 148), Christmas Day until the Eve of Epiphany (p. 157), Ash Wednesday until the Saturday after the Fourth Sunday in Lent (p. 163), The Annunciation of Our Lord (p. 165), the Fifth Sunday of Lent until the Wednesday of Holy Week (p. 167), Ascension Day (p. 173) and the Day after Ascension Day until the Day of Pentecost (p. 175); based on (or excerpted from) *The Roman Sacramentary*.

The Methodist Publishing House: for Prayers after Communion no. 1 (p. 151), from *The Methodist Service Book* © 1975 Trustees for Methodist Church Purposes.

The Saint Andrew Press, Edinburgh: for Prayers after Communion no. 3 (p. 151), from *The Book of Common Order* © Church of Scotland Panel on Worship.

SPCK: for the extended preface for the day of Pentecost (p. 175); taken from *Enriching the Christian Year* by Michael Perham.

sample